Comedia Series ● No – 31

UNDERSTAINS

THE SENSE
AND SEDUCTION
OF ADVERTISING

By Kathy Myers

Comedia Publishing Group was set up to investigate and monitor the media in Britain and abroad. The aim of the project is to provide basic information, investigate problem areas, and to share the experiences of those working in the field, while encouraging debate about the future development of the media. The opinions expressed in the books in the Comedia series are those of the authors, and do not necessarily reflect the views of Comedia. For a list of other Comedia titles see back of book.

First published in 1986 by Comedia Publishing Group
9 Poland Street, London W1V 3DG.

First published 1986

ISBN 0906 890 985 (paperback)
ISBN 0906 890 977 (hardback)

Cover Design by The Fish Family

Typeset by Photosetting, 6 Foundry House, Stars Lane, Yeovil,
Somerset BA20 1NL (0935) 23684
Printed in Great Britain by Unwin Brothers Ltd., The Gresham Press,
Old Woking, Surrey

Trade Distribution by George Philips,
Arndale Rd.,Lineside Industrial Estate,
Littlehampton, W. Sussex.

Contents

HOME SWEET HOME

"There is a spot of earth supremely blest,
A dearer, sweeter spot than all the rest."

OUTSIDE the wind has cried itself to sleep. The brief winter twilight is fading into night and in the deepening dusk the lighted street lamps bloom like giant jonquils.

In the silence and the safety of this firelit room there's a memory and a promise for those thousands far away. This friendly hearth, this shining room remind us that while men make houses women make homes. In the quiet welcome of this peaceful room how easy to forget you're in a house, and only know that you're at home. And how much this happy room owes to little things : to a little care with gentle Silvo : to linens made lustrous white by that last rinse in Reckitt's Blue; to Zebo's winning way with gloomy grates ; and to copper and brass all laughing and gay because of Brasso.

INTRODUCTION

SINCE THE DEFEAT of the Labour Party at the 1983 general election, we have witnessed a transformation in the left's thinking about its public image. Gradually weaned off the soap box as the only effective form of communication, supporters of the political left have flirted openly with the mass media – the GLC splattering its intentions across London's hoardings, the Labour Party splicing together a party political broadcast featuring pop music, a rejuvenated Neil Kinnock and troubadour Billy Bragg – not to mention the flurry of grass roots activity that has spawned a fistful of political dramas and documentaries for Channel Four.

On the principle of fighting fire with fire, it would appear that the GLC and Labour Party at least have decided to tackle head on the cosmetic surgery which Saatchi and Saatchi worked for Mrs Thatcher. In the process they have acknowledged not only the persuasive power of new technologies and the media, but also the necessity of pouring hard-pressed resources into "image making" – previously regarded as an economic luxury, now increasingly perceived as a political necessity.

The trend established by Dwight Eisenhower in the 1952 US Presidential election to sell politics like detergent has run a smoother path in the States than in the UK. Here there is a strong belief that a "good" product, be it commercial or political, doesn't need a salesman to promote it. The British left, hand in hand with the moral majority, has poured scorn on this "Americanisation" of grass roots politics – not least because the advertising industry itself is perceived as decadent and corrupt. Again and again we can see a strange alliance between British puritanism and the broad left – an alliance that has outlawed advertising from the field of "healthy" politics.

The decision, then, of British left-wing institutions to use "commercial"/bad advertising for a "good"/non-commercial political cause, like saving the GLC, has not been

Picture opposite:

HOME SWEET HOME. That hearth-hugging place where all consumer durables eventually end up on the table. If the Empire builders colonised the Third World as a source of cheap labour and raw materials, then advertising, faced by the 1930s with an Empire on the verge of collapse, can be credited with colonising the home. This invasion of the private space would finally put the Englishman's castle on the map, erecting woman to the giddy heights of housewife: as the advertising industry courted her with their consuming passions, and promises of a brighter commodity-soaked future, Silvo, Reckitt's Blue, Brasso and Zebo helped keep the dream clean.

an easy one. Still lurking in the background are the justifiable fears that the real aim of advertising – the handmaiden of capitalism – is to accelerate the rate of surplus value and hive off profit for private benefit. The weak-spirited public are encouraged to acquire unnecessary objects like dish washers, electric tooth brushes and dog hoovers. Gillian Dyer, in *Advertising as Communication*, describes advertising as promoting "private acquisition and competitiveness as a primary goal in life, at the expense of less tangible rewards like better health care and social services."

But even when advertising has been used to good effect, promoting health, welfare and more recently the caring, sharing GLC, it has still met with criticism. Not this time over profit but over language. From both sides of the political fence the rhetoric of advertising – that manipulative "magic" system which appeals to our emotions instead of our logic – has been outlawed as subversive and dangerous. As Gillian Dyer comments, advertising is "an irrational system which appeals to our emotions and to anti-social feelings which have nothing to do with the goods on offer."

To condemn advertising for inspiring an irrationality of emotion is a spurious and dangerous argument. It can equally well be argued that the aim of political rhetoric is to inspire the passions and the emotions. The battle over the political importance of art has always been fought over its capacity to move and inspire – causing grown men to weep and so on. Facts, logic and rationality are not the only way forward. On the other hand, to defend advertising as the "art of the people" is perhaps to miss the point. Advertising today has one primary aim: the promotion of the private accumulation of profit. And the quest for profit to a large extent determines what is for sale, the price of goods and, by extension, the kind of images which we see. Arguably, profit and the politics of promise are indivisible.

The left has always seen both advertising and the accumulation of private profit as political. This runs against the grain of commonsense thinking, which assumes that only propaganda conveys an overtly political message. However, this position becomes harder to defend in the face of any political party's attempts to market politics like detergent. From Kitchener in World War One through Dwight Eisenhower in the 1950s to Saatchi and Saatchi in the 1980s, the West has a long tradition of using advertising methods to further political ends. Clearly the distinction between advertising and propaganda is at best blurred, and one of the aims of this book will be to examine the connections and differences.

In addition to arguments about the economics of advertising and its Garden of Eden serpent's tongue, there is the belief that it's selling us something we don't really need – the dog hoover syndrome. The idea that there are certain basic things which we "need", and that "want" is synonymous with greed, probably only applies in the most limited of peasant/nomadic economies. Even so, the outlawing of "want" as excessive is an arrogant move. Out with the bath water of greed and garden gnomes goes art, entertainment, body adornment, culture and creativity. After all, we don't need any of those things to stay alive. Herds of wildebeest manage well enough without them, why shouldn't we?

* * * * * *

It can be seen from this that many reservations about advertising are based on the assumption of "natural man"; that beneath the gloss and avarice of a consumer society there exists a set of basic needs and wants. As Gillian Dyer comments in *Advertising as Communication*: "The more abundant goods become and the more removed they are from basic physical and social needs the more open we are to appeals which are psychologically grounded ... The reason that we have to be 'magically' induced to buy

things through fantasy situations and satisfactions is because advertisers cannot rely on rational argument to sell their goods in sufficient quantity." The argument is two-fold. First, that capitalism produces a glut of goods which we don't "really" need and, as a follow on, advertising is a form of "perverted" communication which doesn't always tell the truth in its bid to maximise company profits and shift goods off shelves. As Dyer sceptically continues: "The primary function of advertising is, we are told, to introduce a wide range of consumer goods to the public and thus support the free market economy, but it is clearly not its only role; over the years it has become more and more involved in the manipulation of social values and attitudes, and less concerned with the communication of essential information and services."

I want to argue the opposite: that the image of natural man with "basic" needs is as banal as the idea of innocent communication just about facts. Yet the idea of basic needs is an assumption which informs the structure of the welfare state as well as the basic premises of Christianity and the justifiable criticism of the accumulation of profit. Like Darwin in reverse, the argument runs that if we stripped away the artifice of capitalism, natural man would emerge

74% OF LONDONERS ARE AGAINST ABOLISHING THE G.L.C. WHAT'S THE GOVERNMENT DOING ABOUT IT?

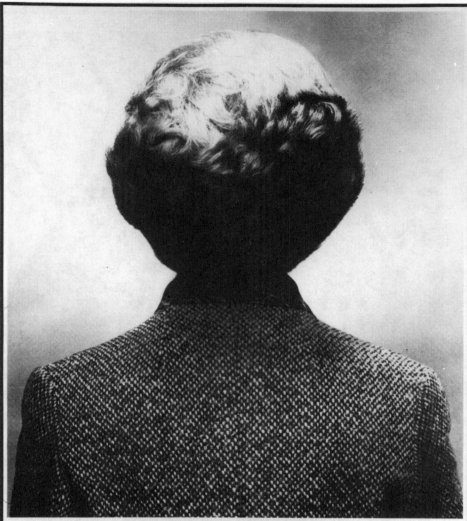

THAT'S WHAT.

The final stage in the Government's plans to abolish the GLC was announced in the Queen's speech yesterday.

Their Abolition Bill goes before Parliament this session.

If it's passed, the organisation that's been running London democratically for almost a century will be scrapped.

And most of its responsibilities won't go to the boroughs as the Government claims but to Whitehall quangos and joint boards which aren't directly elected.

All this will happen in spite of the fact that it's against the wishes of an overwhelming 74% of Londoners.

Understandably, they want to keep the right to decide for themselves at the ballot box who runs London.

The Government obviously isn't interested in what they want. It's pushing ahead with its proposals because it suits them to.

It's an insult to the people of London.

And it's up to every MP who believes in democratic government to vote against it.

In a democracy a government is there to act on behalf of the people who elected it.

Not to turn its back and ignore them. **SAY NO TO NO SAY.**

RESEARCH INDICATES Four in Five of the
Under—50's will suffer more than a year's unemployment during their working lives.
COVER YOURSELF WITH MAKNO'S INSURGENCY PLAN

pristine and untainted: the ape, the innocent, Adam before the fig leaf and Eve's tempting consumer perishables. And it can be readily seen that a lot of left-wing commonsense thinking is shot through with such ideas, a Calvinist belief in thrift and the "true" human spirit; the Protestant work ethic walking hand in hand with trade union demands to "gizza job". Too much pleasure, leisure and comfort corrupts the spirit.

This belief in natural man also ran riot through the social philanthropy and political economy of the 19th century, nowhere more pronounced than in the writings of Karl Marx. Useful things, according to Marx's explanation, are objects without the social gloss – necessary things untainted by style, fashion, taste or social value. Bread, iron, wheat, blankets, water and heating all come to mind as objects which are "basically" necessary to keep natural man fuelled for the road. The problem comes when we start to ask questions about how consumers make "rational" choices between goods which have an identical use value – for example, six different coats, central heating as opposed to coal fires. When assessing advertising, this is where the problem starts: style, fashion, brands all have pejorative associations – different versions of the same "basic" commodity prepackaged and marketed to "gull" the consumer into buying more than they really need.

But whilst the Marxist left conducted a century-long battle against capitalism's fostering of false needs and desires in natural man, the right wing of economics took a different stance. The "Marginal Utility" theorists, represented by economists such as Jeveons, Menger and Walras, were busy pioneering "Rational Man", the replacement for natural man. As Gamble and Walton explain in *Capitalism in Crisis*: "This new theory of value stated simply that value only had one dimension. Commodities no longer had both a value in use and a value in exchange. Their value was only the subjective valuation which individuals placed upon them – the degree of utility they possessed for each individual. Markets were composed of economic agents acting independently, pursuing the greatest possible 'utility' by maximising their returns and minimising their costs... rational behaviour meant maximising benefits. The subjective preferences of all individuals together added up to consumer demand."

So whilst natural man was out hacking the logs, rational man was cruising round the supermarket with a pocket calculator weighing up the relative merits of one brand of detergent against another. But

Picture opposite:

The anarchist *Smile*: **A Journal Of Reactionary ideas, published by The Bonfire Press. If Benson and Hedges replace a gold fish with a gold fag packet, then** *Smile* **takes it one stage further. Two Molotov cocktails are now the golden promise.**

if natural man is an unreal assessment of the consumer freed from ideology and advertising, so too is rational man. Look into any house and it's patently clear that very few purchasing choices are made "rationally" in an economic sense. Many people buy expensive branded goods to make them feel better, throw away unfinished packets of food, and dress in clothes that don't suit them. Not surprisingly, this contrary consumer evidence has always created a problem for positive economics' assessment of the usefulness of advertising. Whilst positive economics argues that advertising is an "aid" to the supply demand equation, informing consumers of their choices, easing the flow of distribution and pioneering the cause of new goods about to enter the market place, it is also patently clear that rational man does not necessarily make rational choices on the basis of this information.

All these idiosyncracies of human behaviour which don't fit with the image of rational man are hived off by positive economics as a statistical variable conveniently labelled consumer tastes and preferences. And, ironically, both positive economics and Marxist economics share a similarly confused vision of the consumer – Marxism explaining away the lack of rationality behind consumer acts as ideology or false consciousness, positive economics referring to the subjective individual area of taste. Both schools of economics effectively outlaw the consumer from their field of enquiry, Marxism by privileging production over consumption, thus further separating the realm of "hard" economic materialism from the more nebulous area of ideology, and positive economics by stating that "tastes and preferences" are outside the realm of scientific economics.

In economic terms it was left to Keynes and his followers in the 1930s to overhaul and reposition a theory of consumption which made the act of consumer choice central to the economic equation, specifically the need to stimulate demand and avert the underconsumption which leads to economic depressions. No accident, then, that advertising as we know it was shaped as an industry in the USA and UK during the 1930s Depression, when the key issue was demand management: the capacity to regulate and predict levels of consumption. Branding, target marketing, product competition, campaigns – the familiar language of advertising – all evolved during this period when rational man had been successfully honed down to natural man and the economy was at a standstill.

The link between advertising and the need to maintain demand, and by extension investment in industry, was explained in the *Introduction to Advertising* (Brewster and Palmer, 1935): "In times of adversity, manufacturers frequently discontinue advertising because it is an expense that can be easily eliminated. When business improves, the volume of advertising increases. One of the beneficent results of the Depression has been an improvement in the quality of advertising since 1929. Today it contains more real selling power and gives consumers more reasons why they should buy. Advertising needs no defence. It is a vital and indispensible part of our system of distribution."

What this advertising handbook and Keynesian economics have in common is a complete disregard for the concepts of natural and rational man. As the Depression illustrated to their satisfaction, even basic wants and needs have to be advertised. And in the 1930s the State took hold of the idea of demand management, advertising such basic commodities as potatoes and coal, trying to flush more money into the economy and out of the consumer's savings tin.

Whilst Keynesian economics as the saviour of the economy has since been discredited, it's no accident that many neo-marxists like Paul Sweezey should reassess the implications of Keynesian demand management for theories of crisis in monopoly capitalism. The points to be made from Sweezey's reinvestigation of Keynes are twofold. First that any theory of advanced capitalism must embrace a sophisticated theory of consumption – which by extension embraces the role played by advertising and marketing. Secondly, the need to look at commodities and their uses in such a way that does not falsely discriminate between "basic" necessary goods with a universal use value, and commodities which have a socially prescribed identity through exchange value. Such a distinction not only makes false claims about "basic" goods, but also resurrects the myth of natural man, the peasant outside culture and society. For it is only by clearing away the "myths" that surround the "magic" of advertising that it's possible to see a way forward, a way for the left to capitalise on the skills and sophistication of advertising and marketing without falling foul of the economic and emotional arguments which currently identify it as tantamount to devil worship.

*   *   *   *   *   *

In this book I shall look at the history and economic function of advertising. Taking a series of case studies, it will be possible to see how advertising pictures the consumer, and how it uses language and images to give products identities. The second part of the book is a survey of the left's criticisms of advertising, and why there is as yet no theory of consumption.

The final part traces the course taken by three "social-ist" institutions which for a variety of reasons have em-ployed advertising to promote their political beliefs and economic objectives. The list-ings magazine *City Limits* is used as an example of a left publication which needs com-mercially to survive on ad-vertising revenue, whilst the GLC and Labour Party are examined as examples of institutions which have used advertising as a favoured means for communicating with the public.

Finally, I've put together some recommendations and suggestions for advertising and consumption in the future. For unless we can ensure the right of the individual to choose what they want to buy, and what kind of lifestyle they want to pursue, then Orwell's bleak vision of "1984" will still remain a prospect for the future.

BANG GOES ANOTHER KIDNEY UNIT.

A kidney unit costs about £15,000. They won't say what an air-to-air missile costs. But a simple anti-tank missile is about £7,000.

And it's not just kidney units that are going up in smoke.

The Government spends nearly eight times as much on defence research as medical research.

And that's the least of your worries.

Newly built hospitals are keeping wards shut because the Government won't give them enough money to run properly.

Since 1979 Government policies have forced 90 hospitals to close down.

Over 13,000 beds have gone out of the window since 1979. Common sense will tell you there aren't 13,000 fewer sick people.

If everyone who's waiting for an operation were to stand in one long queue, it would stretch for close on 200 miles.

But none of this really has to happen.

This Government claims we haven't got any more money to increase spending on the health service.

Want to know the real truth?

It just isn't high enough on their list to warrant the extra cash that's needed.

Defence is. And that is why from 1981 to 1984 spending on defence will have risen by 30%.

For a country that isn't supposed to have any money, don't you think it's amazing what we're spending it on?

Bubbles

BY SIR JOHN MILLAIS BART. P.R.A.

FROM THE ORIGINAL IN THE POSSESSION OF A & F PEARS LTD
(PROPRIETORS OF PEARS SOAP)

1

THE GROWTH OF ADVERTISING:
From "branding" to "target markets"

THE HISTORY OF advertising is frequently recorded as an aesthetic experience: coffee table books groan under the weight of full-page glossy photographs detailing the shift from eighteenth-century cramped classifieds for lost dogs, ponies and slaves through to turn-of-the century pictures of lush Pears babies slipping off bubbles. By the law of natural progression, and the accumulation of "products" in the market place, we end up with an explosion of visual excess and avant-garde art by the 1980s. Benson and Hedges cats paw out glittering gold-fish – a gold pack of fags has become an embodiment of the people's art. This law of natural aesthetic progression conceals, however, most of the economic and structural changes to take place in the advertising industry over the last century. Despite frequent claims that advertising goes back to Moses on the mount, Greek proclamations and Roman street hawkers, the industry as we know it in fact took shape in the latter part of the nineteenth century.

Between the mid-1850s and the late 1890s, the Victorian economy witnessed several major transformations. Popular memory paints this period as one of massive expansion, industrial excess and exploitation, when Britain's Imperial crown ruled the world. According to this image, advertising is the product of an economy lush with money, resources and luxury goods. In fact, the birth of advertising as we know it today stems from this period's very instability of economy; it testifies to an attempt to stage manage the laws of the market place, and

Picture opposite:

The picture book image of advertising. Millais' cherubic innocent blowing bubbles on behalf of Pears soap conceals the rot which had beset the advertising industry by the late 19th century. Advertising, alongside quack medicines, side shows and vaudeville, was regarded as cheap and vulgar. Only inferior products which 'couldn't sell themselves' needed advertising. Millais' bubbles was an attempt to upgrade the image of advertising, in this case by crudely associating the superior quality of the product with "fine" art.

Pictures opposite:

1904 in Bauttes Hors d'oeuvres

19th century advertising, although illustrative, was by today's standards crude. Modern advertising is characterised by an ''understanding'' of the consumer. Ad jargon abounds with terms like consumer orientation, target market, ball point age group and the like. But a century ago the consumer was left out of the marketing mix. Advertisers saw their job as coming up with the most artful, accurate and entertaining set of claims for the product. This obsession with the inherent qualities of the product would dominate marketing rhetoric until the depression of the 1930s, when the consumer finally came into focus.

18

to regulate and stimulate demand at a time of industrial crisis.

By the 1870s Britain, although still the world's wealthiest country, was facing economic and commercial challenge from overseas. Geoffrey Best describes the depression of 1873 in these terms: "The conditions of international trade became less attractive for Britain. Prices, which had risen steadily since 1851, faltered and actually began to fall. What had for thirty years and more seemed regular, stable markets for staple British manufacturers showed signs of saturation. Worse still, British manufacturers were now encountering... competition from the United States, from Belgium, France and Germany." (*Mid-Victorian Britain, 1851–70*)

The impact of overseas competition forced British industry to close ranks. In what was called the "Great Depression", firms which had been brought through the early industrialisation of the century by zealous families and entrepreneurs, gave way to mergers and joint stock companies. In short, there was a shift from private capitalism, characterised by a host of small, highly competitive companies, towards monopoly capitalism, where a few large organisations dominated the market place. "By the third quarter of the nineteenth century there were undoubtedly a great number of tradi-

tional family firms who were experiencing difficulties adapting to competition from newly industrialised countries such as the USA and Germany. Instead of seeking new growth outlets by diversifying their product range, many firms became increasingly specialised, making articles to detailed local specifications as demanded by their customers abroad, and intent on exploring marginal differences in quality." (*Business and Society*, Kempner, MacMillan and Hawkins)

This lack of expansion into new markets, with a resulting intensification and consolidation of existing production processes, precipitated a need for the new monopolies to control the market for their goods. The 1880s and 1890s witnessed mergers within many major commodities – tobacco, tea, beer and baking, for example – a commercial inbreeding commented on by Kempner, MacMillan and Hawkins: "In the Calico Printers Association, for example, formed in 1899 by the amalgamation of fifty-nine firms, the board of directors totalled eighty-four of which nine were managing directors." Similar tales are reported about Portland Cement, Guinness, Whitbread, Charrington, Courage, Spillers and other monopolies formed out of the cannibalistic consumption of small, floundering but potentially competitive companies.

Picture above:

Even by the turn of the century, advertising was still limited primarily to the sale of domestic goods, food stuffs and the services provided by department stores. In 1907, Edward Grove advertised his department store in St John The Evangelist Parish Magazine, - **a temperate little pamphlet littered with simple unillustrated classified ads for printers, piano makers, artificial teeth, matchless teas and other items essential to a God-fearing life.**

From the mid-nineteenth century onwards, advertising therefore began to play an increasingly crucial role in the regulation and stimulation of social demand. This accords with the arguments of economist Maynard Keynes who, almost fifty years later in *The General Theory of Employment, Interest and Money*, set out the case for demand stimulation during periods of economic recession. It also fits with accounts of the 1880s recession, when a period of under consumption went hand in hand with massive pressure by advertisers for the government to relax controls on press and hoarding advertising.

Despite structural changes in the nineteenth-century economy, however, the advertising game was still led by the old faithfuls: toiletries, quack remedies, potions, lotions and soaps. Arguably, these "novelties", with few functional uses, and with many similar competitors fighting for the market, had to be heavily promoted during periods of recession and expansion. For example, the need to brand "Pears" soap as an identifiable product stems from the 1850s, when the market was flooded with a mass of unidentified makes of soap produced by a plethora of small companies. Competition between makes of soap grew throughout the latter part of the century, and leading companies were forced to embark on more ruthless and effective selling methods. By 1880 Pears were spending up to £40,000 a year on advertising; in the 1890s they and Lever Brothers together spent £100,000.

Although target marketing – the tailoring of advertising to a specific social group characterised by class, age and gender – had not yet been properly introduced, it is still possible by the 1880s to perceive the emergence of embryonic marketing strategies. These ranged from the streamlining of distribution (transport, selection of retail outlets) through to the selective packaging and advertising of a product with an eye not only for the other competing goods but also the needs, desires and interests of the potential consumer. In addition, more products began to be branded, and the novelty market of lotions and potions swelled to accommodate a range of foodstuffs: Bovril, Frys, Kelloggs, Nestlés and Hovis all became patented brand names. Products were also given "personalities" the consumers could relate to.

The commercial needs of advertisers to address a wider audience was also facilitated by the 1855 abolition of Stamp Duty, which enabled the circulations of newspapers rapidly to increase and new titles to be founded. Editors were still reluctant to break with the tradition of lay-out that only allowed for classified advertisements and minimal display, and it is partly due to these restrictions that many companies turned to billboards as a way of reaching consumers. The pressure on newspapers to adapt to techniques drawn from the poster was completed by the 1880s, when newspapers like *The Times* and *Daily Mail* started to run large illustrated advertisements.

But perhaps the most pertinent shift in marketing strategy was effected by the advertising industry itself, which moved out of newspaper offices to work directly for commercial customers, offering on their behalf to sell and selectively place advertisements and thus "reach" the most cost effective relevant audience.

By 1900, the agencies had stopped selling space in newspapers completely, thus confirming the shift in their alliance from the communications to the manufacturing system.

The shift from text to illustration mentioned above also revealed advertising's need to engage with a broad mass audience in order to sell basic household products. Several educational philanthropists of the time commented wryly that working-class children were receiving their literary education from the Bovril, Pears and Cadbury hoardings rather than the

Sunday School bible text. And the entry of the working classes – and specifically women – into the advertising market was particularly significant. If Britain could not find markets abroad then it would develop them at home. The domestic purse became the battleground for the fruits of industry.

* * * * * *

Just as the Depression of the 1870s acted as the economic incentive behind product branding, it was the Depression of the 1930s which witnessed the introduction of sophisticated "target marketing". Over the intervening sixty years the rhetoric and presence of advertising had advanced considerably. The Great War of 1914 is often credited with the creation of political propaganda. And precisely the same emotional techniques would later be deployed on the minds of the civilian population by an advertising industry keen to push them into the front line of consumption.

That infamous piece of Great War propaganda, "What Did *You* Do In The Great War Daddy?", is frequently invoked as the father of emotive advertising. Featuring a depressed, emasculated father slumped in an armchair, with a coquettish little seven-year-old innocent nestled in his lap, this image of inadequacy would be churned out time and again in different guises in an attempt to lure parents to buy household goods ranging from the ubiquitous soap powder to food, medicines and insurance.

As Gillian Dyer aptly comments: "One way of getting people to buy vast quantities of goods, and thus to close the gap between the rate of industrial growth and people's purchasing power, was to offer credit and allow people to purchase things by instalment. But this did not really make long term, lifelong consumers out of people, so more manipulative methods had to be devised. People had to be made to feel guilty if they did not buy a new car or radio set, and were taught that it was unpatriotic not to discard things every year in order to buy the latest model of any item."

By the Depression of the 1930s, there was agreement between economists and politicians alike that the best solution for the country was to consume its way out of crisis. A 1931 edition of *Advertising Weekly* blandly stated: "Rising unemployment figures, it seemed, were inevitably reducing our market; yet we refused to be intimidated by this. Consideration of the matter showed that even those who drew unemployment benefit represented a potential market and one likely to be productive enough if approached in the right way. So instead of neglecting the unemployed, we visualise them as a prospective market of 2,500,000 people."

The perception of the lowest wage bracket as a viable economic market marked a dramatic shift from the advertising philosophy of the nineteenth century. Psychological/emotive advertising, perfected during The Great War, was not enough; markets (people) had to be identified as well as products (brands). Only then could "psychological" advertising be truly effective. Clearly soap could not be sold to the affluent bourgeoisie in the same language used to address the worker.

A contemporary guide for the advertising profession, *Posters and Showcards* by Compton Bennett, advised the following: "Advertisements have to be addressed to a certain class of people; the very modern drawing goes right over the heads of a large percentage of the public, whilst the crude, blatant, or pretty-pretty picture makes another class of the public recoil. Again, certain commodities appeal only to certain classes, very few having a really general market... Our so-called 'working classes' cannot afford Elizabeth Arden beauty preparations, and super luxury cars; therefore, they are advertised in a manner which will appeal to the moneyed class. Beers have a wider public, but the vast majority of the consumers of beer are the people who prefer the obvious; therefore, you find beer advertising, on the whole, is generally more crude."

This commercial need to differentiate between markets in time affected media buying policies, and newspapers and magazines began to produce readership profiles with which to attract prospective advertisers. Women's weeklies, the *Picture Post*, daily papers and poster hoardings would all compete for advertising revenue in their bid to offer vast slices of the working population to advertisers. Readers were reconstituted in marketing terms as potential "consumers". And whilst the bourgeoisie continued to provide an important market for industry, from the Great War onwards it would be the working classes, employed and unemployed, who would constitute the bulk of the market.

So if brand "quality" and superiority was top of the advertising agenda in the 1880s, by the 1930s this had been overtaken by the importance of market and "class". Compton Bennett punches home the point: "Before you commence design, you must be sure as to the class of public to whom you have to appeal. You must then try to put yourself in the mind of the buyer, and imagine the type of person likely to buy the product you are handling, in order to find out what qualities will influence him to buy."

By 1931, advertising as a

Picture above:

As the recession of the 1930s bit deeper, even basic goods like vegetables and coal had to be branded and advertised to keep up sales.

profession was selling itself hard to industry. In their *Introduction To Advertising*, a text book aimed at company managers, Brewster and Palmer state categorically: "Advertising increases distribution. It brings before the public the advantages of buying goods or services offered. It awakens new desires and inspires consumers to work harder in order to earn money to satisfy such desires. Advertising is mass selling, without which mass production could not function. It makes possible larger production and lower manufacturing costs. It enables a manufacturer to extend his market speedily and to place his goods in stores all over the country and in many cases all over the world in a short space of time." Crucially, advertising was trying hard to shed its popular image as nuisance/luxury/promoter of novelties and arguing its case for a central role in economic planning: the mediator of production and consumption. In professional terms this meant a shift from the industry as art/design based to being economic/science based. Advertising started to sell itself on the strength of marketing skills and product research as opposed to illustration and the simple buying of newspaper space.

If nineteenth-century thinking was premised on the existence of a "natural" pre-existing market for a product, an audience whose attention simply had to be grabbed to turn them into consumers, then the rigours of the 1930s Depression made it clear that advertising had to construct as opposed to "discover" markets. Branding meant giving the product an identity, target marketing meant selecting a suitable market, and "positioning" the product meant emphasising the qualities of the commodity most likely to appeal to the selected audience. "Desire" became a technical term: more important than rationality or intellect, it was perceived as the motivating force behind purchasing power: "Even when judgement is supposed to dominate completely, the final impulse originates in some deep but unrecognised desire. So that any advertiser might conceivably convince everybody that his article was perfection itself and still starve for orders. Almost every family in the United States has an automobile – at any rate, more families have automobiles than bath tubs, telephones, radios or electric helps for toiling housewives. That is because they desire automobiles; their emotions are involved." (Goode)

The role of women as providers and consumers was particularly central to the new marketing campaigns of the 1930s. Whether or not families had high disposable incomes, industry recognised the need to compete for the sale of even "basic" branded goods like butter, lard, bread and tinned goods. The image of woman as consumer also fitted with the moral and economic climate of the time, with a feminist movement against the exploitation of women in the workplace turning into an emphasis on the role of mother and housekeeper over and above her productive role in the market place. The image of woman as wife and mother equally added grist to the trade union movement's claim that women selling their labour undercut male wages and the strength of the union movement.

At an ideological level the shift from work to home as the correct place for women to fulfil their social duties was effected through the redefining of domestic work as a productive activity. Women's magazines, health guides, cookery books as well as "official" welfare all advocated the return of the woman to the home where she could productively cook, clean, care and consume on behalf of the family. The message is stated loud and clear in Dr Courtenay Beale's *The Perfect Wife*, a 1930 "Health Promotion" leaflet: "Generally speaking, a wife running a home and family on a moderate income, with a little domestic help, had better resist the temptation of becoming a 'public woman'; she has her job, and cannot afford to treat it as a spare time one."

Wives are also advised by Courtenay Beale to drop any feminist connections: "Militant feminists are generally masculine women, nursing a sense of grievance against the sex to which they ought to have belonged, with a certain harshness of manner which can be pretty exasperating; and a man may well feel that such a friend is likely to exercise an injurious influence over his wife, to make her discontented and to stir her into antagonism to himself." And whilst the moral backlash was advocating female passivity, it was in the same breath advocating strength of character in the kitchen. Consuming became a science analysed by hygienists, dieticians, magazine editorials and advertisers alike. The home was to be organised and reorganised on almost a weekly basis to accommodate new "insights" in hygiene and child care, new brands of food and new innovations in cleanliness. Consumption was defined as a full-time, productive activity.

Constipation, that most private of ailments, symbolised the extent to which advertising, the welfare system and the cult of women's magazines colluded to turn even the act of defecation into a science which needed to be monitored and managed by "mother". Magazines such as *Woman and Home* ran a plethora of laxative ads and stirring editorials pointing to the evils

The Most Convenient Way to Buy Your
★LAXATIVE

is in handy-sized tins which slip easily into vest pocket or handbag. 7½d. & 1/-.

Unlike many laxatives, 'Lixen' is entirely free from harsh chemicals which cause painful griping and severe purging. Easy and pleasant to take, yet gentle and effective in action.

'Lixen' Laxative Lozenges have a delicious blackcurrant flavour — children take them eagerly. From all chemists.

Made by Allen & Hanburys Ltd., London, E.C.2.

★

'LIXEN'

The **Natural** Pure Vegetable Laxative

Barry has *boundless* energy

He's a lively little fellow—brimming over with fun. It would be difficult to find a more sturdy, robust boy at his age.

Mother is proud of him and has always kept a watchful eye on his health. She well knows that when needed, a dose of 'California Syrup of Figs' will soon correct stomach upsets and regulate the system.

It is the natural treatment for children—the laxative they like. 'California Syrup of Figs' keeps them regular, well and happy.

"California Syrup of Figs"

Betty and Jane in trouble again

Betty woke up with a coated tongue / and Jane had a feverish headache / and they quarrelled all day long

THAT EVENING NURSE JOHNSON GIVES SOME GOOD ADVICE

BUT SURELY CONSTIPATION COULDN'T MAKE THEM SO NAUGHTY AND OUT OF SORTS?

MY DEAR! OF COURSE IT COULD. WHY! CLOGGED BOWELS POISON A CHILD'S WHOLE SYSTEM.... I'LL JUST SLIP ROUND TO THE CHEMIST AND GET SOMETHING TO PUT THEM RIGHT!

BUT MUMMY SAYS MEDICINES MAKE US WORSE

AH! THAT'S BECAUSE YOU'VE NEVER HAD 'CALIFORNIA SYRUP OF FIGS'

IT TASTES LOVELY

NURSE JOHNSON CALLS IN TWO WEEKS LATER

BUT THEY NEVER QUARREL NOW! IT'S WONDERFUL HOW ONE DOSE A WEEK OF 'CALIFORNIA SYRUP OF FIGS' KEEPS THEM FROM GETTING CONSTIPATED.

Nature provides a simple remedy for irregular and unhealthy bowel action and constipation. The only 'medicine' needed is 'California Syrup of Figs.' Doctors and Nurses recommend this brand of fruit laxative because it stimulates a child's sluggish colon muscles to work *naturally*.
IMPORTANT TO MOTHERS—Safety First! Avoid cheap and drastic laxatives. 'California Syrup of Figs' is absolutely free from synthetic and harmful chemical purgatives. It is a pure fruit laxative and gives natural aid to bowel action. It is, therefore, ALWAYS SAFE, even for the youngest babe. Of all chemists 1/3 and 2/6 with full directions. When buying be sure to get 'California Syrup of Figs' brand.

"California Syrup of Figs" BRAND
'NATURE'S OWN' LAXATIVE

of tight-bowelled children, wives and husbands. The lower colon was seen as a potential home wrecker. "Nurse Johnson" stops two little blighters from running into the juvenile courts by administering California Syrup of Figs. In the same issue, Kellogg's All-bran, the roughage dam buster, promises to "bring back your husband's sunny disposition", thus saving a marriage. Meanwhile, a contemporary health pamphlet made no bones about the evils of blocked bowels: "What is known as frigidity in women – their indifference or aversion to marital relations – is often traceable to just one cause. Habitual constipation is both a disgusting and a dangerous condition, which no healthy minded woman should tolerate."

It can be argued that the 1930s therefore witnessed the introduction of the marketing methods and psychological selling techniques familiar today. The need to "get consumers to commodities", as one advertising manual put it, marked a sharp departure from the problem of distribution – getting commodities to consumers – which had characterised earlier phases of the economy both in Britain and the United States. This need to "deliver" audiences to advertisers meant that marketing refined its use of specific advertising mediums, employing such resources as the ABC (Audit Bureau of Circulations), which gave independent details of magazine and newspapers' circulation, readership, subscription rates and other details important for successful target marketing. But as well as the refinement of existing selling techniques, the 1930s in the States also witnessed the arrival of a new and powerful medium: radio.

* * * * * *

Whilst the BBC in Britain was dedicated to Public Service Broadcasting – the Director General, John Reith, writing in 1931 that "The BBC must lead, not follow its listeners" – the American system started off in pursuit of commercial profit. During the Depression, radio was perfect in providing a captive audience for commercials and the sponsored "soaps": radio shows thus named because of their sponsorship by detergent manufacturers. The soap and cooking oil conglomerate Proctor and Gamble, for instance, had invested two million dollars in radio soaps by 1935. In 1939 the company had twenty-one serials under its sponsorship worth 8¾ million dollars. As Peter Buckman comments in *All For Love*: "Daytime radio consisted of easy music and talks of beauty, better laundry methods, and how to make lighter pastry. The advertisers were not slow to realise that these captive women – the domestic slave market – were

Good sailors are their own doctors. That's why ashore or afloat this is my standing order

A.S.

– every morning take

ENO'S "FRUIT SALT"

2/- and 3/6 a bottle (tax inc.)

This R.A.F. Cadet writes:

There is something "different" about Eucryl, what it is I don't know but am completely satisfied to accept it

EUCRYL
TOOTH POWDER

IN TINS   9d. & 1/3

also the main buyers of household goods."

The impact of radio in colonising the domestic market cannot be under-estimated. Contemporary statistics (1930) estimated radio ownership in the States at 18,000,000 "radio homes", all the more crucial in a semi-literate population packed with immigrants scarcely conversant with the American mother tongue. In order to maintain the credibility of the advertisements, handbooks at the time advised businesses only to invest in radio stations which employ announcers of "the highest quality". "Announcers must be men of education and culture and able to use the English language correctly." (*Introduction to Advertising*, Brewster and Palmer.)

During the day the radio dished up housewives; in the evening, with a carefully constructed "family" policy, it aimed to reach men still in employment and kids sufficiently old to blackmail their parents into buying certain branded goods, like sweets and flavoured toothpaste. Advertisements were scheduled to run up against programmes most likely to seduce the intended market: music, sport and current affairs for the men, soap and womanly advice for the women. The attraction of radio was emphasised in *Introduction To Advertising*: "As of April 1930, radio owners paid eighty-four

per cent more rent per family than non radio owners. Radio owners owned homes seventy-nine per cent more costly than non radio owners. The typical radio family earned ninety-three per cent more income than the typical non radio family. Radio ownership is everywhere broadcast in the upper income levels and descends like a wedge into the low income levels. The average radio family contains more consumers, more gainful workers, and more adult listeners than the average non radio family."

By contrast, the commercial invasion of the airwaves was banned in Britain, "chaotic" freedom of enterprise ousted in favour of "order and organisation". The Sykes and Crawford Committee, which reported on the matter as early as 1923, asserted that "the range and functions of broadcasting in the fields of entertainment, culture and education, its social and political possibilities, and its power over public opinion" called for a single broadcasting service in the hands of a public corporation ultimately responsible to parliament and the government of the day. The press colluded with this wave of public responsibility, concerned – as today – that commercialisation of the BBC might undercut their advertising revenue.

This vehement anti-advertising stance did not, however,

prevent the government from using the radio for advertising purposes during the Second World War – under the guise of the Ministry of Information. The radio series *The Archers* was pioneered as a way of getting across farming information and over £7,000,000 was spent on press and poster advertising during the War. The costs fell in three fields: special announcements on rationing etc., long-term campaigns designed to adjust the population to the war-time economy (National Savings, Ministry of Food, Agriculture and Fuel), and finally political propaganda. The last included The Empire Campaign produced by the Ministry of Information and the Ministry of Health's drive against VD. Government advertising thus saw the promotion of "demand management" in reverse; whilst the 1930s had incited consumers to purchase more, the war economy demanded that they consume less. But despite the difference in objective, the emotive language coined during the Depression of the 1930s was still allowed full head.

Perhaps the most interesting aspect of this period was the shift in the image of women in advertisements. As Gillian Dyer explains: "Since women were so vital to the economy outside, as well as inside the home during the war, the advertising images underwent a fundamental change. Instead of being shown as passive consumers mainly interested in their appearance and the shine on their furniture, women in wartime ads were depicted more realistically as bus drivers, factory workers ... Products such as soap, convenience foods and household gadgets were offered as a source of help to busy women rather than as avenues to greater social status or as a means of relieving guilt feelings."

The War still inevitably hit commercial advertising. The rationing of newsprint had a double effect, on the one hand greatly reducing the size of all publications and on the other compelling a severe reduction in the space allotted to advertisements; and although rates for advertising were substantially increased, this was not enough to make up for the reduction in volume. The net revenue of the press was 12.5% lower in 1943 than in 1935, but whereas revenue from sales had increased by 27.5%, revenue from advertisements declined by 40%.

The impact of government advertising during the War cannot be underestimated, however. Deploying the talents of many commercial agencies, the rhetoric of government advertising was to lodge skilfully between propaganda and public relations – an elision sometimes portrayed in more glorious terms: "Everyone wants to be in the movement for a better world – a planned world – of peace and

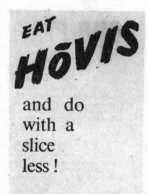

EAT
HŌVIS

and do
with a
slice
less !

BEST BAKERS BAKE IT   *Macclesfield*

KODAK FILM
is in the Factories
**helping to ensure flawless
aircraft parts**

Illustration shows an aircraft engine cylinder head about to be X-rayed. Internal faults in the casting which might prove disastrous in operation will be revealed on the film before the part is assembled. Next time you have difficulty in getting a spool of 'Kodak' Film, remember it is because such vital work must come first.

Kodak Limited, Kodak House, Kingsway, London, W.C.2   F.316

**Pictures opposite
and above:**

Advertising joined in the war effort with gusto. Whilst rations might restrict sales, defending the home front did wonders for the corporate image of brands like Hovis.

Pictures above:

War talk was used to sell women commodities during and briefly after 1945. But their image as sensible rational producers and consumers would rapidly be usurped by the flurry of femininity as advertising and the country colluded in a conspiracy which suggested that all women had ever really wanted to do was breed, bake and beautify their bodies.

plenty and fair shares for all. More than any other branch of modern business, advertising, in the service of private profit, has attracted the contemptuous criticism of the moralists and the high minded social philosophers of our day. Advertising people are acutely conscious of the fact. Here, then, it seems, is their chance at last. Here is their opportunity to fit into the brave new world of purpose and high endeavour; to join the ranks of the planners and the 'directors of the good society', and to play their part in the psychological guidance of the masses.'' (Bishop, *Ethics of Advertising*) Stirring stuff, written at the close of the War, when the brave new world was just tipping over the horizon. And it showed how, in less than a decade, advertising had become honourable, shifting its motivation from private profit to public welfare.

The end of the War also witnessed a peculiar battle in advertising between two images of womanhood. Many advertisements played on the remembered strength of women as war workers. Main gas cookers promoted their product with the slogan: ''She's been using the finest equipment in war. She'll want the best equipment in peace.'' By contrast, beauty product manufacturers were presenting the newly won War as a ghastly plague against the body, wrinkling femininity and

ruining hairdos. As Ferguson Fabrics put it: ''Transformation: Home At Last! No more barracks, no more drill, no more uniform, and a wardrobe of pretty, pre-call up Ferguson frocks, still as fresh as paint and crisp as lettuces.'' But perhaps one of the most overt tactics of the post-War era was to banish the ''make do'' thrift in favour of branding. By 1946 most goods were still rationed and few available in the shops. This didn't stop advertisers like Horlicks, Ponds Cream, Ferguson Fabrics, Creda domestic appliances and Lil-lets from placing ads in magazines asking women to ''hold on'' until the brands reappeared in the shops. Ponds warned: ''It is indeed a problem – whether or not you should take an unfamiliar brand of face cream when you can't get Ponds... and when you do get Ponds, you'll find it pays to use it sparingly rather than to experiment with unknown face creams.''

The re-appearance of branding, and the rapid shift in the image of women from worker to housewife, testified to the sensitivity of marketing skills to the prevailing social climate. Advertising, directly harnessed to the political economy during the War period in a concerted national bid to manage consumption patterns, was loath to relinquish the power and skills it had acquired.

* * * * *

In 1949, Bishop's *Ethics of Advertising* held out great hope for the promise and potential of commercial advertising. With the nationalist flag waving, he celebrated the industry's Dunkirk spirit that had led the people through the War and would offer "psychological guidance to the masses" in the quest for "The Brave New World". Bishop predicted that, following the fate of fascism, the new economic enemy for Britain would be Uncle Sam: "It is imperative that British salesmanship abroad, including market reseach and direct consumer advertising, should be of the highest competitive quality. Yet here we are at a grievous disadvantage. The greatest economic fact in the modern world is the colossal productive power of American industry. This power has been built up by the methods of mass production, supported by the development of modern sales technique to a degree that has left Britain and every other country far behind."

British advertising, Bishop argued, should be mustered in support of the export drive abroad, and on the home front to raise the standards of living, aspirations and moral tone of a population crushed by the weariness of a war decade. Advertising, the great leveller, by providing information for all, was at the forefront of democracy, a symbol of the Allied victory. With a final flourish, Bishop called for more than "technical" ability: "Advertising needs leaders of the widest culture and experience," he wrote. Advertising must become a profession.

Seven years later, Vance Packard in *The Hidden Persuaders* (1957) presented a chilling vision of this Brave New World gone sour. Advertising, handmaiden of the war effort, was now portrayed as the henchman of industry, battling ruthlessly for the purses of consumers. Emotional advertising had become blackmail. Psychological appeal had turned into brainwashing. Information was little more than indoctrination. Packard introduced his sermon on consumerism with the following: "This book ... is about the way many of us are being influenced and manipulated – far more than we realise – in the patterns of our everyday lives. Large scale efforts are being made, often with impressive success, to channel our unthinking habits, our purchasing decisions, and our thought processes by the use of insights gleaned from psychiatry and the social sciences. ... The use of mass psychoanalysis to guide campaigns of persuasion has become the basis of a multi-million dollar industry."

Whilst Packard's impression of the mindless consumer, culled and gulled by advertising, was overstated, his book did point to the manifold ways in which "motivation" re-

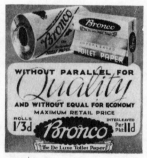

Pictures above:
Maintaining brand loyalty in the post-war period.

search had become a mainstay of the selling industry. Martin Mayer, in the equally influential *Madison Avenue USA*, written the following year, was scathing of Packard's hypothesis: "Packard classifies as motivation research the entire work of the advertising business, from copy writer's horse-sense hunches (Ted Bates' 'Clean your breath while it cleans your teeth', attributed by Packard to motivation research done some sixteen years after the slogan made its first appearance) through to Dichter's most rigorously Freudian analyses. And such confusions, of course, are the wellsprings of controversy."

Even so, Mayer was the first to argue that advances in psychology had affected selling methods in advertising. He suggested that it was the crisis in orthodox 'head counting' sociology which had precipitated this need. Agencies such as the American McCann Erickson were busy pioneering the relevance of "in depth" psychological research as against the use of simplistic demographic data: "The common failure to deduce market characteristics from breakdowns of demographic data, coupled with the discovery that many housewives actually did not know why they bought one brand rather than another, produced demand for psychological classifications, for the discovery of the 'real reasons' which guided consumers in their choice of brands."

In practice, most agencies favoured the psychological and sociological approach to consumer research. Status symbols as a register of class aspiration mingled with Freudian accounts of desire and personality in the bid to sell more. Mayer noted wryly: "Advertisers are impatient with the niceties of difference between theoretical disciplines and any research firm which announced that it could do one branch of 'projective' research but couldn't do another would shortly find its clients dribbling to a firm which offered both for the price of one."

Most of the "motivation" research with which we are now familiar was pioneered during this period in the United States, whose economy had survived the ravages of World War Two to better advantage than the UK. There, the crisis of over production was already in full swing whilst Britain was still struggling on ration cards. But as the British economy blossomed, the skills of American selling were inevitably imported. One of the key concepts coined in 1950s American advertising which still survives today is that of "lifestyle". In a country which had fought for Independence over the issue of democracy and meritocracy, "lifestyle" was an acceptable euphemism for class. In Britain, too, it was an appealing concept for a country which had recently

NOW YOU'RE ENGAGED

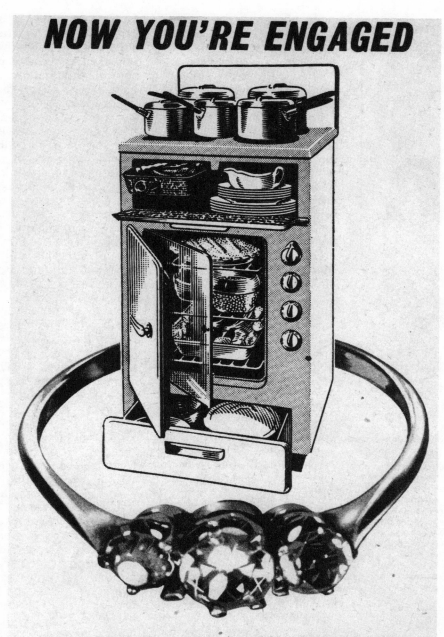

Now is the time to think about the things you must have to
start a home of your own. A cooker, for instance. Go along to your

1951

1951

Pictures opposite and above:

The 1950s witnessed the birth of the teenager. If *Housewife* magazine in 1951 had depicted the post-war pubescent adolescent as a cross between Bambi and a honey bear, *17* magazine would, a few years later, groom and prune the same child into a sexual, commercially sane mini-adult. By 1967, *Jackie* magazine aimed at the weenie end of the teen market and had replaced talk of school japes with "groovy girls" who mixed with "Beautiful People". such as Gordon Moore's improved Joan Meredith.

voted in a Labour government, trouncing the class-riddled paternalism of Churchill.

Psychology and sociology fleshed out lifestyle, building on the assumptions not of how people actually lived, but how they wanted to live. Aspiration was a key ingredient. More sophisticated than the "Star-let" advertising of the 1930s which relied on a famous face to sell fags, furniture and cold cream, lifestyle tailored social origin to aspiration. Keeping up/ahead of the Joneses was an essential ingredient. Reference/peer groups were now thought to provide the basis for accurate aspirational research. Such thinking was embodied in the American advertising sociology of such writers as William H. Whyte, who in 1956 produced the seminal guide to white collar suburban aspiration: *The Organisation Man*.

Whyte's acid pen talked about the crises of "keeping down with the Joneses" as suburbanites "inconspicuously consumed" their way into community acceptability. Suburban dwellings, like brands of soap, are near identical. The art is to inscribe difference without seeming flash or vulgar. The wrong car in the wrong colour could precipitate the ulcer-inducing tag "not quite our sort of people". The art of inconspicuous consumption means that "it is the group that determines when a luxury becomes a necessity. This takes place when there

comes together a sort of critical mass. In the early stages, when only a few of the housewives in the block have, say, an automatic dryer, the word of mouth praise for its indispensability is restricted. But then, as time goes on and the adjacent housewives follow suit, in a mounting ratio others are exposed to more and more talk about its benefits. Soon the non-possession of the item becomes an anti-social act – an unspoken aspersion of the other's judgement or taste... Item by item, the process is constantly repeated, and the norm never stays still. As soon as a certain range of items becomes standard in the neighbourhood group, its members grow restive for a new necessity."

The insights of *Organisation Man*-style analysis, together with the commercial imperative of shifting more goods to more consumers, meant that the concept of "total marketing" came to the fore. In 1957, the British Market Research Society was formed, representing twenty-odd market research agencies and 120 delegates. And the industry rapidly grew, offering research on consumer preferences to the product development wing of industry and to advertising agencies. This eventually developed into the provision of continuous syndicated services: retail audits, consumer test panels, qualitative "ad response" research, etc. By the end of the 1960s this embryonic business was turning over £17 million.

The indispensability of marketing was recognised by a major Labour Party report on advertising, published in 1962. Stating the position of the IPA (Institute of Practitioners in Advertising), the report explained: "Marketing ... encompasses determination of size and price, shape and design of package, deploying and paying manufacturers' sales representatives, setting wholesalers' and retailers' trade margins, arrangement of display at point of sale, provision of guarantees and after-sales service and advertising." Advertising had become a subdivision of a much more important enterprise.

The shift in marketing technique from an obsession with distribution to an investment in consumption also meant that people's actual purchasing patterns had to be observed more closely. In the United States at least, selling more each year was perceived as essential to national growth, full employment and a satisfactory balance of payments; and with the exception of overseas sales, selling more meant getting each individual to purchase more. Several solutions were offered, starting with the creation of "fresh" markets for a product.

The possibility of developing new markets depends on the process of "market segmentation". This means dividing the total pool of people into smaller and smaller groups, either by virtue of their basic age, gender and race or by virtue of their lifestyle. This is a complicated process which often goes hand in hand with new product development. For example, Maltesers have over the last twenty years been marketed to different segments of the female chocolate buying public – oscillating between a "no mess" appeal for white gloved mums and a "slimming aid" for young girls. The latter campaign depended crucially on dropping the fatty chocolate overtones which fettered the brand image of Maltesers. Hence "Chocolates? No, Maltesers!"

A classic 1950s example of market segmentation in response to the demands of industry was the creation of the "teen-ager". During the War boys grew up into young men, girls became mademoiselles briefly for the benefit of pubescent dress patterns and, then, with a great sigh of busty relief, became women. Magazines of the early 1950s charted in great detail how mothers might turn their "leggy" female offspring into "real women", a process which revolved around posture, cleanliness, putting the hair UP, letting the skirt DOWN, wearing heels and crossing the legs. James Dean was one of the first publicly disaffected teenagers: as a "brand leader" he was also crucial to the concept that the teenager, and especially the

1959

seventeen

OCTOBER 1955
35 CENTS IN U.S. AND CANADA
40 CENTS ELSEWHERE

THE
SEVENTEEN
LOOK
and where
to find it

male of the species, was culturally, aesthetically, politically and financially at odds with the parental generation who bred babies for "The Brave New World".

In the States, *17* and *Glamour* magazine, alongside *Madmoiselle*, were the first youth magazines to take the teenager economically seriously. The founders of *17* sold the teenager as a concept of the marketing man, and as back up for their new protegée they produced a bulk of "educational" material: packs, films, booklets giving advice on hygiene, dress sense, career opportunities. And if the teenager of the early 1950s was advised in *Housewife* magazine to keep off daddy's lap as training for "welcoming guests with a smile and a handshake", *17*'s teenager was (by 1959) going on dates: "Since your audience is as close as the face of the boy holding you on the dance floor or the boy sitting next to you in the snack shops after a movie, your date-time make up should always be carefully rehearsed and then double checked... Does your eye shadow show above your lids? Do you look a bit pale? Even rosie by day beauties may need a touch of rouge at night."[29] Grooming was commodity intensive. "Basic Props" for the reader of *17* ran to twenty-seven items, including a small artist's brush and three shades of lipstick. More stuff than her mother might have seen in a lifetime spent in Depressions, recessions and war economies.

By the late 1950s the concept of the teenager was an accepted part of marketing rhetoric, and *17* magazine began to produce vast market research reports for potential advertisers. In 1968 this 100-page, fully illustrated dossier came up with the following claims for the average teenager: "They're rich. They take their own money (total $7.1 billion annually) and spend it on everything from fun to furniture, clothes, cosmetics. With dad in his peak income years they can persuade him to provide cash for big ticket items: as a result 925,000 drive their own automobiles. They bank in their own accounts (63.6% in savings, 12.8% checking). And when they run short of cash, they simply say 'charge it please'. 5.5 million present mother's plate. 850 show their own."

Embryonic market research was also to reiterate what the advertising industry already knew: that since the beginning of the War, women had been responsible for making the majority of "domestic consumption" decisions. Whilst the 1950s economy had demanded that they relinquish their new found independence and return to the sanctity of the home to cook, clean, childcare and caress their husbands' work-wearied brow, women maintained their role as principal decision-maker. Whilst hubby might

LIPS

1. Shape not well-defined? Outline lips in a fairly dark shade of lipstick. Fill in with a lighter shade. Blend carefully.

2. One lip too thin? Use a light lipstick on the thinner lip and a slightly darker shade (avoid too much contrast) on full lip.

Pictures above:

Full time femininity. *17*'s **Advanced Beauty Workshop, 1959.**

. . . I knew you'd like it, darling

Frock in pure wool, trimmed silk £5 . 12 . 8. *(Packing and postage 1/6d.)*
One of many attractive models from our range

I found this pretty frock in the Maternity Department at Treasure Cot to-day.
Then I asked their advice on a really good belt and the layette.
They were so helpful and seemed to enjoy planning as much as I did.
Mother's buying the pram there, and Father the cot, so now
you must come and see the Nursery Furniture.
I can't wait to show you what they've got—you'll be as excited as I was.

Treasure Cot

Treasure Cot Catalogues of mothers' needs: **M.** Maternity Wear
A. Clothes and Equipment for a new baby **E.** Toddlers' Wear, 3 months to 2 years
C. Children's Fashions, 2 to 8 years **F.** Furnishing the Nursery
Please send for these booklets price 2½d. each post free

TREASURE COT · 103 OXFORD STREET · LONDON W.1

shell out for the "big" items like cars, washing machines and lawn mowers, it became patently clear that the wife's approval was essential. Admen were faced with the difficult task of making domestic hardware ads which appealed to the aesthetic and economy of the wife while representing a sturdy status investment for the husband. Many 1950s ads for cookers, cleaning equipment and new look kitchens endorsed the maxim "You know who wears the trousers", but a "wise wife" never lets her husband know. Part of the appeal of these ads was their conspiratorial feel: women may have stopped welding but they still knew how to wield power and their husbands' wallets.

The refinement of marketing techniques in the 1950s, coupled with the economic potential of developing "new" markets, was supported by a long term industrial drive to get people to consume "more" of a particular commodity. One car families became two car families. TVs popped up in the living room, kitchen and study. This year's fashion collection reproduced at a rate of knots into this season's collection. Food, drink, make up and shoes became seasonal. This "intensification" of consumption is still a feature of contemporary marketing, but there's a limit to how many cars a drive will park or how many Crimson Ice shades of lipstick you can pack into a top drawer. Vance Packard des-

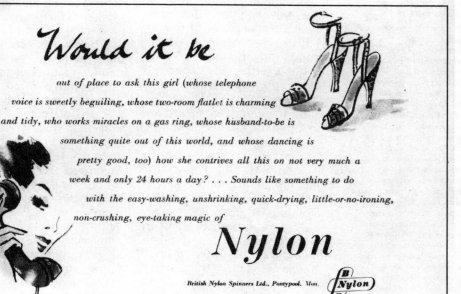

Would it be

out of place to ask this girl (whose telephone voice is sweetly beguiling, whose two-room flatlet is charming and tidy, who works miracles on a gas ring, whose husband-to-be is something quite out of this world, and whose dancing is pretty good, too) how she contrives all this on not very much a week and only 24 hours a day? . . . Sounds like something to do with the easy-washing, unshrinking, quick-drying, little-or-no-ironing, non-crushing, eye-taking magic of

Nylon

British Nylon Spinners Ltd., Pontypool, Mon.

Picture opposite:

The 1950s was the decade of conspicuous consumption. The American economy, on the edge of a crisis precipitated by over production, threw itself whole-heartedly into the act of selling. "Built in obsolescence", a term disparagingly coined by Vance Packard, referred to the American obsession with building things that wouldn't last, either aesthetically or practically. The aim was to get the average citizen and his family to consume more each year. As William H. Whyte acidly commented on the mid American male: "The wrong car in the wrong colour could precipitate the ulcer-inducing tag: not quite our sort of people."

cribed this 1950s phenomenon as "the nagging prospect of saturation".

This fear was to be realised in the late 1950s when a commodity glut followed the worst recession since the 1930s. Unemployment and piles of unsold furniture rose simultaneously; and the market reacted to the challenge of the mounting glut by shifting to the hard sell. In Michigan sales executives were reported to have fired a cannon each time a car was sold. President Eisenhower came up with the solution, "Buy Anything", to make the recession recede. Buying became a patriotic duty, with the economists – full flush with Keynesian demand management rhetoric – convinced that government and consumer spending was the only solution. But whatever the real cause of the late 1950s recession, it undermined advertising and marketing's faith in the capacity of an economy endlessly to consume more of the same.

By 1960 Vance Packard was to hold up for public inquiry that most "insidious" aspect of marketing: "planned obsolescence", the rapid outmoding of a good or service due to breakdown, fashion dictates or cost. Cars, light bulbs, matchstick furniture were all built to fail. Replacement was the way forward. But perhaps more than shoddy construction, which could rebound on the production company, fashion, style and

taste started to dictate the desirable lifespan of an object. Being "out of fashion" or "non-modern" was, by the early 1960s, a death sentence for a product.

Big cosmetic companies like Revlon, Max Factor, Elizabeth Arden and Helena Rubinstein quickly learned the lessons of planned obsolescence. This year's colour was accelerated to this season's colour, with further diversification dependent upon the blonde, brunette or auburn tones of the consumer. At a slower pace, the schedule of obsolescence moved out of the fashion/novelty cosmetic market into hardware and consumer durables. Today, the annual overhaul of aesthetics and "customer benefit" in cars, dishwashers, electrical equipment and furniture is standard practice.

From the advertising agencies' point of view, product quality, uniqueness of function or attractive price could no longer provide the mainstay of advertising copy. Few goods were unique, most brands competing in a similar market, selling in the same supermarket to near identical customers, a tendency accelerated by 1950s business mergers into conglomerates and oligopolies. With a few major companies dominating the market, and spending most of the advertising revenue, the market could have been reduced to a few major brands. In fact, as the car and soap powder

It Gives a Man a New Outlook...

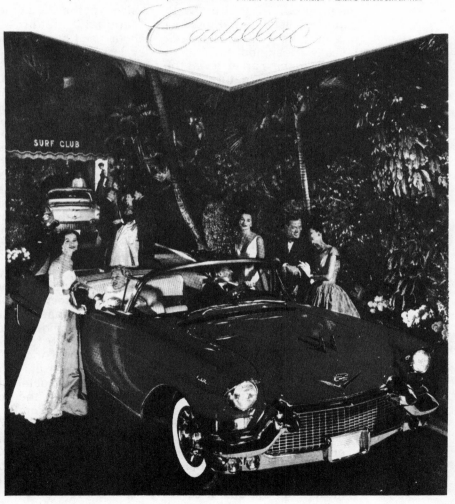

...when he first views the world through the windshield of his own Cadillac car. There is the wholly new sense of pride he feels as he sits in possession of a motor car that is so widely respected. There is the entirely new feeling of mastery he enjoys as he puts the car through its brilliant paces for the very first time. And, finally, there is his deep pleasure in realizing that he has made one of motordom's soundest investments. And, of course, all of these sentiments will be all the more pronounced for the motorist who makes the move to Cadillac in 1957. Why not visit your dealer and see for yourself? You're welcome to try the view from the driver's seat at any time.

CADILLAC MOTOR CAR DIVISION • GENERAL MOTORS CORPORATION

Cadillac

SURF CLUB

41

industries testify, the opposite was to occur. Large manufacturers produced a range of near identical commodities, brands which would compete against each other for shelf space, each pitched at a different consumer group. Advertising and marketing agencies, in league with industrialists, started "product development": products specifically designed to "fit" a "gap" in the market. It was the death of the "natural" consumer. If a market didn't exist it would be artificially created.

* * * * * *

In the run up to the Wilson government of 1964 the Labour Party report already mentioned reveals the dilemma of socialist strategies within a system of expansionist commodity capitalism. With the new world rhetoric of the late 1940s abandoned, advertising – clearly no longer a "public information" industry – was regarded as a necessary evil. As the report pointed out, the "meritorious" procedure of providing information "is not always practicable". "The exigencies of competition and the real difficulty of making a new product, or improving an existing one, so as to achieve an obvious and readily perceptible benefit, can put the agency in a position where it is employed to advertise products which are not leaders in the market...Here the agency must... do the best it can to get the product sold. The result can all too easily be irrelevant product differentiation, excessive protestations of merit, and far-fetched reasons why the product should be believed to possess chosen characteristics."

Several other features of advertising were raised in the Party report. Firstly, there was concern at the massive level of "national" resources and labour used by advertising, a level of expense which "cannot be justified in terms of the information it provides the consumer." The commission also decided that oligopolies and monopolies benefited most from advertising, through profitable sales, "without any corresponding gain in productive efficiency". They simply passed on the cost of expensive advertising to the consumer, protected from price cutting open market competition through their monopoly hold on the resources of the industry. Finally, the report concluded that successful "product branding" effectively marginalised the competition in the consumer's mind. This observation was substantiated by investigation of the cigarette industry, "where the immense obstacles facing potential new competitors and the conservation of abnormally high profit levels are due principally to the power of advertising."

Despite the economic insights of the earlier sections, the commission, chaired by the BBC's veteran Lord Reith, was to make at best cosmetic suggestions to the Labour

Party, which was in government by the time it appeared. Its recommendations included the establishing of a National Consumer Board to monitor complaints and invest money in product research and tests, and the maintenance of the Advertising Standards Association as a voluntary watchdog. The report did include, however, a scathing attack on the newest medium to be made available to advertisers – commercial television. Lord Reith was reported to consider the introduction of commercial television to be "one of the most unfortunate and indeed pernicious decisions ever taken by a government, from which an immense amount of ill has already accrued, presumably with much more to come."

Reith's parallel prediction that commercial television was not wanted proved inaccurate. As the number of television sets had risen through the 1950s so, too, had advertising revenue. In its first year (1956) ITV took £10.6 million (3.4% of total advertising revenue). By 1963 the figures had risen respectively to £85 million and 16.9% of advertising revenue. To its relief, press revenue from advertising had not dropped substantially, testifying to the optimists' belief that Britain was supporting a burgeoning economy.

Commercial television was (and still is) regarded as one of the most cost effective means of reaching a mass audience. Colloquially known in the advertising industry as "the blunt instrument", TV has often been criticised for its crude market research. The result of this theoretical poverty is that TV commercials have tended to favour the eye-catching "shot gun" approach to advertising: general appeal because they can't be sure who's watching. Only in recent years, with the advent of Channel Four, have the TV monitoring groups, such as BARB (Broadcasting Audience Research Board), made any attempt to refine their measurement techniques. Channel Four is the first British TV attempt to target market ads to tie in with specific "interest" programmes – gardening programmes supported by greenhouse ads, pop programmes by record commercials and weepy afternoon dramas by cosmetics and toiletries.

In the 1960s, however, the emphasis of those concerned about the power of advertising was on the equal power of the consumer to discriminate. This attention to "customer detail" ran from Reith's attempt to establish a Consumer Council through to the overhauling of supermarkets, checkout counters, HP facilities and even town planning. In 1956 there were a hundred supermarkets in Britain; by 1967 there were 3,000. Hire purchase was easily available, convenience food a necessity of life, over half the population owned a refrigerator and a washing machine. More and more goods were produced by fewer and fewer companies. In 1930 there were over 2,000 small millers; by the mid-1970s that figure had been reduced to thirty. It was the day of the mass-produced white branded sliced loaf. Mothers' Pride was everywhere, rivalled only by Sunblest. Consuming was a twenty-four-hour business and, despite Reith's protestations, TV had rapidly established itself as the primary form of family entertainment and the most "influential" form of advertising. Adverts for coffee and tea during commercial breaks were said to be so effective that the national power grid would slump. In 1961 75% of families had a TV; ten years later the proportion was 90%. And television's slice of the advertising cake rose to over £200 million, leaving newspaper revenue far behind.

Amidst this flurry of finance and expansion, the advertising industry witnessed several significant changes. With the Wilson administration breath-ing down its neck, care was taken to "tighten up" campaigns. But most important was the shift in marketing practice. If the housewife and teenager had been the discoveries of the 1950s, the 1960s represented the rise of the affluent working class: the C1–C2s would now provide the backbone of the economy. Favoured for their propensity to spend, love of cash and HP, coupled with a loathing of "invisible investments" (mortgages, insurance, private medicine and education), the "Dagenham car worker" was the ideal consumer. And it would be to the skilled working man and his family that the bulk of advertising over the next twenty-five years would be directed. These were the people who took holidays, bought new cars every couple of years, bought convenience food, followed the fashion in drink and ditched gear as soon as it was too long, too short or too colourful. For the first time the working classes were regarded as an asset to the consumer economy.

Picture opposite:

1962 and the pre-packed, pre-cooked, almost pre-digested meal had already arrived. A labour-saving device, aimed at the housewife and geared to convince her that meals in packets would liberate her... more time to do the rest of the housework and work an eight-hour day. It was the beginning of a consumer revolution which rapidly relined the average gut. The working-class diet, spiced by American, Indian, Chinese and Italian ersatz cuisine, would never be the same again.

Fabulous Chow Mein in 15 minutes—prepared by Vesta for you to cook!

You can cook this popular and tasty Chinese meal in just 15 minutes. It's complete: sumptuous Chow Mein with succulent soft noodles, subtle soy sauce and the most delicious *crispy* noodles you ever tasted!

Expert chefs have done all the hard work for you: they've rolled the noodles, chopped the vegetables, prepared the beef, created the wonderful Chow Mein itself. All *you* do is cook it . . . and take the credit!

BMP 13-9672

Serves One 2/3d   Serves Two 3/9d

36

Other adventurous dishes from

VESTA

**BEEF CURRY WITH RICE
VEGETABLE CURRY WITH RICE
SPAGHETTI BOLOGNESE**

2

REASONS TO BE CHEERFUL: ADVERTISING TODAY

1: Why advertise?

ALMOST THIRTY YEARS ago, Martin Mayer (in *Madison Avenue USA*, 1958) described the battle between two schools of advertising thought: the McCann/Greys agency view of "total marketing", and the Ogilvy, Benson, Mather agency's belief in "branding" the name of the product. David Ogilvy of OBM was regarded by Mayer as the "apostle of the brand image, creator of 'The Man in The Hathaway Shirt', populariser of 'The Man from Schweppes', poet of the charms of Puerto Rico." The brand name was everything, the wearer nothing. "Sell the name, and you've sold the product", he was once quoted as saying. Critics from the marketing school of thought were less convinced, describing Ogilvy as a "snob selling products on the appeal of exclusivity and status". The campaigns for Puerto Rico

amplified this. At an Advertising Association meeting he announced: "We want people to think of Puerto Rico as a country of beautiful mountains and romantic beaches, inhabited by brave and friendly people who are equally proud of their Spanish traditions and their American citizenship." A tall order given that most Americans at that time regarded Puerto Rico as a brothel soaked in cheap booze, and inhabited by halfbreds and ex-pats laundering ill-gotten earnings.

By 1978 the OBM agency, in a planning and research report aimed to convince prospective clients that they knew the selling industry inside out, had shifted the emphasis. Product "personification" (branding) had given way to consumer "personification" (target marketing): "It is axiomatic that the creators of advertising,

Picture opposite:

Avon is the world's leading manufacturer and distributor of cosmetics, fragrances and costume jewellry. Founded in 1886 with a single product and one Representative, Avon today offers more than 700 products through 1,200,000 independent Representatives in 30 countries.

Consolidated net sales in 1979 were a record $2.38 billion. Net income of $251 million was also a record. (Avon Annual Report, 1979)

Their success depends on capturing the friendly face of femininity. Potential customers (left) and sales reps (right) encourage "girl next door" familiarity and identification. The key word is "accessible".

concerned with communication, have to think of a typical target consumer... It is equally obvious that the creators of advertising need to know just about everything there is to know about this consumer. They need understanding of the consumer's relationships with the product – how the target consumer thinks and feels about the product and how it is used and the way it fits in with their lives. It is wrong to begin thinking about the brand and its attributes and how to compete with rivals without first thinking of basic consumer requirements and habits and about basic thoughts and beliefs.'' (*A Consumer's View Of How Advertising Works*, OBM, 1978) This shift in agency thinking from brand to buyer illustrates well the impact which thirty years of market research has had on advertising practice.

The availability of a likely target market determines not only the rhetoric of a campaign, but whether a product will be launched at all. In the late 1970s, for example, Tyne Tees was hardly a fashionable area in which to live. But by a peculiar act of demographic fate its small urban population represented a perfect sample of the great British appetite. More unknown chocolate bars have lived and died on the Geordie streets than in any other part of the country. This was also an expensive operation. At that time companies reckoned they needed to spend £1 million to float a new product for up to twelve months. Success could take it down the M1; although the seventy per cent failure rate of new products made this unlikely.

One product to make it from manufacturer to test pitch, and finally to the nation's tastebuds, was "Yorkie". Manufactured by Rowntree Mackintosh, Yorkie is a prime example of a product developed on the strength of consumer research. Unlike competing producers Mars and Cadbury, Rowntree was "weak" in the chocolate bar branch of confectionery. In response to escalating cocoa prices, Mars and Cadbury had also ironed out the chocolate bar into a broader, thinner shape. Market research suggested that consumers were unimpressed, and wanted a bigger bite for their money. Rowntree's response was to develop a small, chunky bar, personified in the ensuing advertising campaign by a coast to coast lorry on a long haul. Names like "Rations" and "Trek" were abandoned in favour of Yorkie, a name that was thought to have wholesome family appeal whilst still being macho enough to pull a man-size bite. Yorkie therefore represented not only an attempt to outmanoeuvre Cadbury and Mars on traditional family ground, but also an effective bid for the male appetite: a potentially large and lucrative market.

The success of campaigns like Yorkie (or Krona margarine) in launching a new product conceals, however, the fact that the majority of advertising aims to sustain the position of *existing* products in the market. To illustrate the point, advertising executives are keen to point out the fate of "Force", a popular cereal in the 1950s which died when starved of advertising. A similar fate befell Delsey toilet paper in the early 1960s. Having seen off the tyranny of market leaders such as Bronco ("it crinkles as it cleans"), Delsey sold itself on the strength of competitive pricing. But without advertising back up, Delsey was overtaken by Andrex. The latter has since been pulled by the super-soft Labrador puppies into a brand lead position, controlling a third of the toilet tissue market.

There are several reasons given for advertising in order to sustain existing sales. As one agency man put it: "Most products on sale don't have a use which couldn't easily be fulfilled by a probably cheaper competitor. Product differentiation is one of the most exacting tasks in advertising." Given that the shelves are glutted with a host of near-identical products, agencies argue that advertising is essential to keep new customers coming along. Guinness, for example, feels the need to advertise all the year round in order to maintain its existing level of sales. The same applies to other major brands such as Kelloggs, Weetabix, Fairy Liquid, etc.

Guinness is also an example of a company which, in order to maintain the product's position, has continually to reassess its share of the market. Throughout the 1970s Guinness' agency, J. Walter Thompson, had made repeated attempts to "spread the load" of the drink's appeal. Getting away from the "old man and his dog" image, the agency presented a series of campaigns which argued that there were more things to do with a pint of stout than write your name on the head. As well as marketing Guinness as a "cooling" lunchtime drink alongside the perennial body builder, campaigns attempted to draw in the women's market. Ads started appearing in magazines like *Cosmopolitan* and *Company*, with professional young women adding half pints of Guinness to their repertoire of social accessories. This tactic of attempting to reach a broader cross-section of the public was not considered successful by the company. The result was that, with the appointment of a new Chairman, J. Walter Thompson were fired and the relatively young agency, Allen, Brady and Marsh, appointed instead.

There then ensued a massive market research campaign which concluded that the correct policy was not one of diversification (seventy per cent of Guinness drinkers drank it only occasionally) but of concentration. ABM decided to pitch Guinness in direct competition with other beers. Research showed that ninety-two per cent of all beer was consumed by men, and that half of these were under thirty-five and working class. The solution was to present Guinness as an "in" hip drink excluding the "Guinless" – blokes who'd gone too long without a pint and had lost their lip/edge. The campaign received a lot of flak, especially from those who thought it below the standards set by JWT. In aesthetic terms this was probably true, but as the aim of ABM was to attract young "street wise" men, the creative shift arguably justified the results. Guinness' first financial report after the campaign showed sales increases of ten per cent.

Perhaps more complex than these processes is the use of advertising to hold back the erosion of a commodity's appeal through consumer over-familiarity or the successful campaigning of competitors. Previously this was regarded as the job of a successful creative team coming up with a "good idea". But agencies now recognise that creative thinking is useless unless harnessed to the insights of the marketing machine. Even with an established product, sample consumer groups are used not only to "test out" the effectiveness of a new ad, but to judge the gulf between the agency/client's impression of the target market and the actual consumers. A case in point is Boots "No. 17" cosmetics. Originally targeted at teenage girls, subsequent research demonstrated that the product range was bought by women of all ages on the grounds of quality and thrift. New campaigns were targeted accordingly, using images more likely to appeal to a wider range of women.

Advertising is used frequently to re-establish the image of a product when it is "re-launched". For many companies this is a perennial activity in the bid to stave off competition. Make up, detergents, petrol, cars and household cleansing agents are all candidates for the "new improved" value-added treatment. Each time an extra ingredient or accessory is lobbed into the marketing mix it gives advertisers justifiable grounds for trumpeting the advantages of the product. This can be simply an attempt to get existing consumers to buy more, seduce purchasers away from competing products, or to increase the product's market share by attracting 'virgin' consumers.

Finally, as in Mel Brooks' "Spring Time For Hitler" in *The Producers*, the aim of advertising can be to *lose* sales. This is the most hotly disputed and least likely area of advertising, but bears consideration. Rumour has it, for example, that in the late 1970s Chanel No. 5 was deliberately promoted through commercials designed to throw most consumers off the scent. Chanel's problem was maintaining exclusivity when they discovered that the C1s and C2s (white collar and skilled workers) were buying it. If the ABs (upper and professional middle classes) got a whiff of that, they'd stop buying it instantly. Overnight they'd be pouring the stuff down the loo and investing in Magriffe, Madame Rochas or Guerlain. Chanel noticed the problem when sales started to go up beyond the annual purchasing capacity of the ABs. After all, there's a limit to how much No.5 the landed gentry can douse on themselves – or their good lady wives – over a year.

Further panic set in when the company realised that the C1–C2s were a faithless bunch when it came to brand loyalty. This year Chanel, next year Arpège. Sales might be doing a bomb at present "with the Dagenham car worker", but the boom could soon be over. The sight of a glut of Chanel in the chemist's window (a fate which befell Revlon's ubiquitous "Charlie" a year earlier) would also act as a major turn-off for the ABs. The restoration of exclusivity was paramount. The solution: a campaign for Chanel which the C1–C2s would find repulsive, yet wouldn't alienate the traditional AB quality market.

Extensive consumer research revealed that the C1–C2s loathed jazz and the avant-garde. A campaign was produced for No.5 (which they fortunately loathed) featuring an icily beautiful couple spinning on a blanched dance floor to the accompaniment of electronic twangs. The couple, a massive car and a Chanel bottle then montaged into one. TV advertising was the chosen medium: expensive, but it had the advantage of catching the C2s whilst the ABs watched a documentary on BBC2.

One other aspect of advertising's job is worth mentioning. New products are often "created" by segmenting the product market, or by interbreeding two existing products. One such example is the "body spray". Invented in the late 1970s, the body spray had the capacity to be a deodorant, a freshener (as in "Evian" water spray) and a cheap perfume. Market research had already demonstrated that each of these three respective markets (deodorant, perfume and waterspray) was glutted. There was no room for a new product. Room was found, however, by combining the functions of all three: the body spray was no longer a smelly deodorant, it was a freshening, deodorising perfume. This much more appealing recipe – with the same constituent ingredients – was launched on the research groups and later gave rise to sprays such as "Impulse". Still marketed on TV today, the picture of a pretty girl accosted by a lad with arms brimming full of flowers – "acting on Impulse" – is a familiar sight. Whereas old-fashioned agency practice perceived branding as a way of capitalising on the product's existing strengths, new-style advertising is paid to set about creating them.

There is also a range of other objectives for advertising apart from those already mentioned. The aim of direct response advertising, for example, is usually dramatically to hit sales targets and shift large quantities of warehouse stored goods. Again, much of the advertising from the public sector doesn't aim to *sell* anything, but simply to create audience awareness on issues such as public safety, health, food, etc.

But none of these disparate forms of advertising – the selling of products, maintenance of existing sales, public information – would work unless the advertiser has a clear impression of who "his product is speaking to." As one account executive put it when quizzed about the launch of an inexpensive fashionable fragrance: "That product might as well not exist unless I know who we're supposed to be selling it to. The client's got fantasies that we can compete with Chanel No.5. Pigs might fly. Anyway, that's a very small select market. What we want is the C1 and C2 nineteen-to-twenty-fives. Girls and young women without too much responsibility and a lot of spare cash. That's the target market."

The prospective "target market" affects all levels of agency decision-making, and a major source of initial information on the nation's spenders is the National Readership Survey. The NRS classification of Social Grades is the most widely used in advertising. It has six descending levels:

A   Higher managerial, administrative or professional.

B   Intermediate managerial, administrative or professional.

C1 Supervisory or clerical and junior managerial, administrative and professional.

C2 Skilled manual.

D   Semi-skilled and unskilled manual.

E   Those at the lowest levels of subsistence, pensioners, widows, casuals and the unemployed.

The NRS survey itself is based on the occupation of the male head of household, or female "housewife" in the case of single parent families. Unlike the similar Registrar General scale, which includes the weighting of income into its fuller social assessment, the NRS survey, based on interviews and collated data, only records information about income. This means that in terms of classification, several anomalies can occur. The most important of these concerns "housewives" who, despite their own background, occupation and social tastes, will be classed according to their husbands. Market researchers quote examples like "the female gynaecologist married to a bus conductor who gets classed as a D housewife." Equally, children and students are graded by their fathers' occupation until they leave home: "So all you need is little Bobby, whose dad is a judge, to move into a shared house and suddenly he's lost his grade A status." The NRS classification also produces mismatches for women traditionally employed in grades beneath their capability, for example secretarial or low level admin. work. Despite their lifestyle and aspirations, they will still be classed as C1.

Even so, the NRS classification by occupation is really a shorthand way of grouping people according to their aspirations, ambitions and lifestyles; and these value judgements are thought, in the end, to provide a more finely tuned assessment of people's spending patterns than sheer hard cash. As a spokesperson for the NRS survey put it: "After all, a retired bank manager, despite his fall in real income, isn't going to stop a life-long passion of buying complete sets of Wagner opera just because he's left his job. On the other hand a car worker with ten times the amount of disposable income might never buy a Wagner record in his entire life."

Classification by occupation also provides the backbone of the other agency "bible" on consumers' habits – TGI (Target Group Index). TGI provides information on consumers' age, sex and region, all geared to a systematic breakdown of how the various groups spend, and linked to the consumption of anything from pet foods to petrol. It is continually updated by the British Market Research Bureau. TGI also marks a sharp departure from traditional commercial thinking where brands of goods are defined by use and function on the presumption that they would find their appropriate consumer, and turns the consumers themselves into marketable commodities which can be "bought" through a specific medium. Magazines and other media in turn effectively function as merchants offering the reader to advertisers.

The trade press, for example, is full of adverts from publishing conglomerates like Thomson's and IPC boasting the "target markets" which their magazines can reach. The following advert was placed by National Magazines in *Campaign* (the advertising trade weekly) in a bid to attract the attention of agencies.

"ABC 1 × 3 million. Spend a month in colour with National Magazines and Cosmopolitan, Harper and Queen,

FLEX PROTECTS!
FROM LIMP, DULL, OVERDRIED HAIR.

Hair dryers. Heated rollers. Sun. Wind. Pollution. Protect your hair from the damage they can do. Flex Instant Conditioner with Balsam and Protein fights back in seconds to restore body, bounce and shine. Makes hair manageable and tangle-free. Beautiful! And to keep hair super clean, try Flex Balsam and Protein Shampoo.

REVLON

Good Housekeeping, She and Company will put you in touch with 33% of all ABC 1 women. Independent, discriminating, intelligent and above all affluent. Britain's most desirable women. Spend six months with National Magazines, and the figures are even more glamorous: 51% of all ABC 1 women; 65% of all ABC 1 women under 35. No other publishing company reaches so many desirable ABC 1 women at so little cost. Be they fashion-conscious younger women, discerning housewives, or decision-making business women. Taken all in all, National Magazines are the best-written, most beautifully designed magazines now available for Britain's ABC 1 women and ABC 1 Advertisers, too."

To support such claims, publishing companies like IPC produce their own research dossiers on the purchasing patterns of their readers.

2: The agency

There is no agreed structure for an advertising agency, and many agencies market themselves to potential clients on the strength of the "unique" service they offer. Apart from size, agencies differ basically on whether they offer a comprehensive marketing service – or farm out consumer research to specialist companies. Many of the larger companies are internationally based, both in terms of their ownership and the clients whose interests they service. A number of UK agencies are hinged to American parent companies: examples include Young and Rubicam, Greys, McCann Erickson, Norman, Craig and Kummel and Ted Bates.

The next section provides a description of the different departments within advertising agencies, and an outline of the functions which they perform.

Account management

Despite the misleading allusion to book-keeping and accountancy, "account management" refers to the overall control of running a campaign on behalf of a particular business, or "account". An account director/manager/executive (in decreasing order of importance) is likely to be a client's first personal contact with an agency. It's up to him – and of recent years also her – to assess the client's advertising/marketing problem and to liaise internally with the various departments of the agency. This dual loyalty to agency and client means inevitably that the accounts department is "where the buck stops". They're the first to take credit, the first to be booted out when a campaign goes wrong.

In the old days this was said to be the habitat of the Oxbridge graduate: the man with

Picture opposite:

The ideal woman of the 1970s in the States was based on the model of Farrah Fawcett Majors and Cheryl Teig. Both renowned for their flowing blonde hair, flashy toothy smiles and friendliness. The image didn't travel. British and German women refused to identify with the Mid West grin.

manners capable of "saying the right thing", smoothing ruffled feathers and keeping the client happy. Nowadays Oxbridge has given way to a broader spectrum of appointments, although still primarily recruited from university, "with a good degree, gift of the gab and ability to squeeze round tight corners." Charm and an ability to "handle a rebellious creative team" run in parallel with a sharp financial sense. Although separate departments within the agency deal with budgeting, accounts and business plans, the account director is ultimately responsible for devising and agreeing the best "media package" for the campaign.

But an account manager's job involves more than a capacity to appease all the interested parties: he has to offer solutions for the client's problem. If the "problem" (reason for advertising) is, for example, falling sales, then it will be the responsibility of the account manager to commission the appropriate research and design a strategy for increasing sales. Hand in hand with the selection of an appropriate target market will go the "positioning of the product".

David Sinclair, formerly of the Norman, Craig, Kummel agency, described the process of "positioning" men's aftershave and skincare products in 1980. At that time the "problem" was to try and break down the assumptions that body lotion was "poofy" or "continental". Research had demonstrated that men surreptitiously did use moisturisers. "The problem was to get them to stop using their girlfriend's baby lotion. We needed to get the C1–C2 men, our main market, to recognise that dry skin was normal and not poofy." Sinclair argued it as a "timing problem". During the glam rock and "punk thing" in the mid-1970s men had worn make up; and in about 1973 there had been an embryonic attempt to launch male skincare products – like the Aramis range – in major department stores. This attempt had been a financial failure. Sinclair was convinced that the reason lay in the men's toiletries market's inability to subvert the "effeminate image" of skincare.

The agency began playing with the idea of a male moisturiser as a "treatment", or alternatively as "après ski". They might even call it that. Rugged, glam and fitting in with the C2s' upwardly mobile aspirations. A C2 full-blooded male wouldn't be embarrased about having "Après Ski" in his bathroom cupboard. In fact the result was called "Mandate", whose new market lay in the consumer waste-land between "toiletry" aftershave and the upmarket "designer fragrances". It was set up to replace Brut, a significant brand shareholder whose image had been eroded and downmarketed by sheer force of popularity. Mandate would be relaunched in the "middle of the road", halfway between the down market products and the dry designer fragrances: aftershave like vintage wine.

The relaunch of Mandate and its successful "halfway" positioning in the market, Sinclair argued, was also contingent on the "incorporation of lifestyle" into the adverts. Lifestyle, the representation of aspirations and class ambitions in commercials, had been used to great effect in the women's toiletries market, but had rarely been tried in the men's market. Sinclair remarked cynically that most aftershave up to that point had relied on simple "surf and sex appeal" to shift the product. Mandate was to be positioned as a "sophisticated sensual fragrance". "Everything expensive is sophisticated," he said.

To illustrate the point he spun off the bakelite-like top of a Chanel bottle. "Feel the weight of that," he said, emphasising the quality of the product. The packaging of Mandate was neat. Gold letters and mock agate finish. Apparently the design came from some kind of vinyl floor or wall covering that had been converted for the job. The bottle, blocky and rectangular, was a bit tacky, however: they'd been left with the design from the previous launch.

But there's another meaning to sophisticated. It refers to the target audience for the launch, in this case the ABs, the top twelve per cent of the population. "Of course we don't really aim at the ABs," Sinclair explained. It seemed they were too small a market to worry about, weren't in the habit of splashing their liquid assets about, and had already been corralled by the "designer" fragrances. But the advantage of "seeming" to pitch a product at the ABs is that the C1 and C2s would aspire to it.

Tailoring the product to make it look AB to the C1 and 2s, but *not* to the ABs, was where the real creative work came in, involving a combination of image, distribution and price. To start with, only the right kind of upmarket chemists/Boots should be allowed to stock Mandate. One of the main brand competitors would be Aramis. This would be signalled to the customer through complementary pricing. And the image they ended up with was Sacha Distel. Sophisticated, good looking, French. Market research showed that women (who did sixty per cent of the buying) loved him. Men didn't actually object to him. The idea was to get the women to buy it, the men to wear it to please them, and consequently rebuy it. The model for Mandate was married, had his own house, thought he was sophisticated and had a way with women.

So what was the clincher which targeted the right market? Sinclair smiled, lit another

Marlboro and rocked back in his chair: "Sacha Distel". It seemed that Distel had C1 not AB appeal. You wouldn't get middle class mums going gooey-eyed over that French lisp. Sinclair also felt that C1 housewives had a "moral" streak which militated against the playboy image of after-shave advertising: "What sensible wife is going to pay for a product which will encourage another woman to run off with her man?" Hence the significance of the last frame in the Mandate TV commercial which shows Distel with his arm around a woman with her back to the camera. Distel looks from the glowing fire, back over his shoulder into the camera and says: "It's alright, she's my wife."

The Mandate campaign could not have been conceived or developed without comprehensive research into the aspirations of the potential target market group. And whilst it is account managers like Sinclair who interpret the data in terms of a campaign strategy and creative brief for the copy writers, the actual research work involved is the responsibility of a separate department within the agency. This is variously termed research, marketing or planning.

Account planners

Account planners, unlike executives, who tend to be culled from industry or direct from university, are trained researchers – skilled in market research, numeracy and a variety of psychological and sociologically based analysis techniques. Peter Hurd, account manager for Boase, Massimi, Pollitt on the GLC anti-abolition campaign, argues that this function is essential. "In an agency such as BMP there simply isn't the time to continually send out for specialist marketing services. We need results very quickly."

Hurd explained that each advert produced for that campaign was sent to sample consumer groups, and only then launched. "It's from that kind of research that we managed to isolate the key issues for the public, for example "democracy: the right to vote". People didn't like the idea of losing their vote. That continuous feedback from consumers meant that we knew when the time was right to shift from, say a serious approach, to the more light-hearted image of the later adverts – for example, the poster bound up in red tape. That idea had been conceived a few months previously, but we had to wait until our research told us that the time was right."

Not all agencies who employ planners use them in the same way as BMP. Frequently they operate in a separate marketing or research department. But research is a massive responsibility for a research planner such as Carol Cootes, who was central to Ogilvy, Benson, Mather's marketing operation for Avon cosmetics.

Avon is not sold retail in shops but "door to door" through a vast network of local representatives – the "Avon ladies". Despite this relatively "low profile" the company has consistently stayed at the top of the cosmetics market. Its market share of face packs, for example, rose to twenty-eight per cent in 1976, leaving the rest of the market trailing behind, and the same commercial domination continues through blushers, nail varnish and lipsticks. This marketing success has been the result of local availability, "the personal" connection built up between rep. and client, and not least Avon's comprehensive understanding of their housewife consumer. But to stave off the competition from companies such as Max Factor, Cootes felt that it was essential to engage in "permanent market assessment. A way to expand the customer base and sell new product ranges to the existing market."

Cootes argued that their research precipitated the company to move away from "lifestyle" advertising (the props of kitchens, gardens, kids and furniture which "give away" the socio-economic intentions of the advert) in favour of the "look". Rather than tying themselves down into a specific class image which could alienate a large proportion of Avon's con-

sumer base, "Colour Me Avon" and similar campaigns concentrated instead on the face. This emphasis on the look is substantiated by the Avon catalogue for 1980, packed with face and product shots against matt coloured backgrounds. No class, status, regional giveaways here.

As Cootes put it: "They don't need us to tell them they're housewifes or suburban mums, which is why for example one of our ads featured a flower shop. Cosmetics give them a chance to step outside their normal domestic situation. What we're offering is the 'Cinderella effect'. For the price of a few cosmetics the possibility of total transformation. So it's really important that the models we use to promote Avon's range are accessible. They mustn't be too glamorous or perfect. It's a confident, outgoing, lively sort of look. They're not painted ladies. Models have to look like a credible girl next door, so that when a woman sees one of the adverts she thinks 'Yes, I could look like that too.'

"A lot of Avon's success is built on the information and brochures which we supply on make up technique. A lot of the women we sell to wouldn't have the nerve to go into a department store and ask the sales assistant for her advice. We might have reached that kind of conclusion by guesswork. In fact I don't believe we could have got that near to the attitudes and aspirations of

Picture on Page 60:

If companies like Avon plumped for the girl next door look, other brand leaders went to the opposite end of the make up counter, favouring the face of sophistication. Revlon, nicely nuzzled in the top half of the market, went for image for image's sake. Audiences weren't to be asked to identify, they were being asked to admire. Being asked to play the role of spectator, as well as potential consumer, is often a feature of more abstract, self-conscious advertising aimed at people who can appreciate the aesthetic implications of surrealism and narcissism.

Picture on Page 61:

Look, no Lifestyle props. Avon advertising carefully avoids coding its adverts with messages which could be read in terms of class, status and social position so as not to alienate any one group. Avon understandably steers away from interior shots: carpets, furniture, fabrics and wall coverings all give tell-tale clues as to the owner's loot level. Instead, the 1980 Avon Catalogue favoured close-up shots of models' faces, and when a location was needed favoured outdoor shots, preferably accompanied by out of focus "mood" backgrounds.

REVLON INVENTS
THE LIPCOLOUR
WITH POSITIVE STAYING POWER

New
Living Lipstick

At last, lipcolour built to last.
Rich in new colour. Rich in new smoothness.
And dramatically longer in colour wear.
Encased most luxuriously.
This is the lipcolour you'll live in and love!

REVLON

HONEYSUCKLE
*The sweet-smelling flower
of early summer*

Roses Roses
The legendary symbol of love

*A garden
of flowers
all the year long*

our consumers without extensive market research, and our sales bear me out on that."

The capacity to come up with this kind of finding means that research planners like Cootes "spend an awful lot of the evenings and mornings in coffee drinking sessions", talking about new ranges, product developments and new make up techniques with sample consumer groups. All this information is analysed, quantified, computed and finally packaged into reports which the account managers can feed to the creative directors in charge of the appearance of the campaign.

The creative department

The creative department actually produces the adverts which we see. This work is done on the basis of a lot of negotiation and the "Creative Briefs" produced by the accounts department in consultation with planners/researchers and the client. An example of this is the Schweppes creative strategy. This lists the advertising objectives, product's positioning, target consumers and principal consumer benefits. The job of the creative team is to visualise these requirements.

Creative departments usually comprise a number of creative "teams", in effect a partnership between a copy writer and an art director. Depending on the scale of the operation, some creative teams will oversee a project from start to finish, including typesetting, finished artwork and the commissioning of photography. More usually there is a greater division of labour, with creative teams organising the original campaign concept and then effectively sub-contracting to artists, illustrators, typographers and photographers to come up with the goods. For TV commercials the creative team will produce a "story board" – a series of cartoon-like freeze frame felt tip illustrations which convey the narrative of the commercial. Once again this will be handed over to video/film making specialists with a creative/art director overseeing the shoot.

In most agencies creative teams rarely come into direct contact with the client, relying on a strong account manager to present their ideas coherently. Some agencies favour a more direct approach, inviting creative teams along to special briefings with the clients. Some teams value this direct involvement, others regarding it as "a crashing bore which means you've got to change your clothes, brush your hair, listen to the account manager pour syrup everywhere and the client ask why the girls have got so many clothes on in the advert. Any account manager who wants me in the room doesn't know his business."

The invective often carries over into the job itself. Many creative teams regard advertising as a health hazard, referring with customary gloom to the number of bright young things who burned out before they reached thirty-five. Of all the departments, the creative teams, although arguably the most important in determining an agency's success, are also the most disgruntled. Tony, for instance, who preferred not to give his name or employer, said that a lot of creative teams comprised frustrated artists and novelists. "We've all got the unfinished masterpiece lying under our beds. Running a copyline for a third rate fridge is no competition." He regarded account executives as a necessary evil: "The men in suits keep the clients at bay." But he could hardly conceal his contempt for clients, reactionary by nature and unimaginative by definition: "A good client is one who doesn't turn up at the agency except to sign cheques." A lot of creative work is described by many teams as "death: little black and white jobs that appear in the dailies – factual, bland and boring." Almost without exception, and not surprisingly, most creative teams prefer something they can get their teeth into, like launching a new product or promoting a more sophisticated or luxury item. Examples of campaigns listed by creative teams as fun included Benson and Hedges, Chanel No.5, quality fashion and cars.

The philosophy of the creative team is understandably at odds with the more "hard nosed" economic imperatives of the account, research and media buying teams. As one art director put it: "The demands on us are very complex. One week we have to be inside the head of Mrs Average in Cheam, and the next we're supposed to think like a top company executive so we can sell him a watch. There's pages of market research to go on, how Mrs so and so thinks, what programmes she watches, etc., but in the end it's my head that matters. I've got to produce the creative art work that not only she'll like, but my Oxbridge inspired account manager will accept and the nouveau riche client will buy. And you wonder why we burn out?"

Media buying

The Media Planning department is probably one of the most important yet least sung areas of agency activity. It is this department which determines how a client's budget will be spent, and where its advertising will be placed. As already noted, one legacy of its former close relationship with the press is that the agency is paid by the media through a commission on space sold – roughly standardised at fifteen per cent. But the media planning department is responsible for more than the simple placing of already executed advertisements. It's involved in campaign strategy from the outset, looking at the creative brief's suggestions for reaching the target audience through press, TV or radio.

With the massive capital investment involved, media planners leave little to chance. Whilst each media strategy is tailored to the requirements of the specific campaign, some things can be budgeted for and planned. For example, certain plum sites in women's magazines will be pitched for well in advance of a campaign because they're "dead certs" in commanding the reader's attention. This applies to the back cover, inside front cover and pages facing editorial matter. Other favoured locations include the space opposite the problem page and horoscopes. Revlon (handled by Greys advertising agency), for instance, operated a monopoly for years on the inside front cover of *Vogue*. Similarly, CDB (Collett, Dickenson and Pearce) discovered in the early 1960s the appeal of double-page spread advertising in the newly launched Sunday supplements, buying space well in advance of need. The same "buying in advance" policy extends to poster and TV advertising.

Much of this process of booking space is science/statistics based. In order to come up with the optimum spread across the three main media (TV, press and radio), the planner must assess three factors: coverage, frequency and cost per thousand. Coverage is defined as the percentage of the target market that will see the campaign at least once. Frequency is the number of times each person will have the opportunity to see, hear or read the campaign. And cost per thousand means the cost of reaching 1,000 members of the target audience. In the case of press advertising this is defined as individuals; with TV the cruder statistic of "homes" is used. Every media schedule combines these three ingredients.

To work out how the maximum percentage of the target audience can be reached most frequently, at the least cost, media planners cross-reference their research. Basic information sources include BARB and JICTAR, which indicate popular TV programmes and viewing ratings, the National Readership Survey for information on a magazine's circulation, readership profile, etc., and TGI (Target Group Index) for a much more sophisticated analysis of such things as the number of people who buy petrol, go on holiday or buy pet food per publication. Take, for example, a product like "Outdoor Girl", a low price make up range aimed at fifteen to twenty-year-olds. Upmarket magazines like *Vogue* and *Harpers* would automatically be out; TGI and NRS would indicate that few of the kind of girls likely to buy Outdoor Girl would buy *Vogue*. Regular women's weeklies, renowned for their broad ad-based readership across class and age, would deliver some of the desired target audience. But a magazine like *19* or *Honey*, themselves aimed at teenagers, would provide a more exact profile and hence a better cost per thousand investment.

An equally important part of the media planner's job is to offer advice on "environment": an advert has to look "at home" in a publication. For many creative teams this presents the headache of making an advert fit in with the "in house" style of a publication, whilst simultaneously making sure that it stands out and is noticed. Media planners also argue that the credibility of an advert often accrues from the "quality" of the surrounding editorial. For this reason adverts are sometimes made to look like editorial for a "rub off" effect. Examples include the Kerastane haircare product adverts looking like the "Irma Kurtz" problem page in *Cosmopolitan* (March, 1980) or the Outdoor Girl advert made to look like an illustration for a magazine story.

This notion of environment balances the importance of cost and target audiences. It might be argued that in simple cost per thousand terms, TV regularly dishes up the best target market deal. After all, among the twelve million viewers watching an early evening soap, there is likely to be a higher percentage of avid gardeners than even the most popular gardening magazine could deliver. But many agencies feel, for example, that women's magazines offer the "right environment" for the sale of toiletries, make up and fashion: they convey more credibility than flash, brash TV commercials. The fact that women pick up, re-read and browse through magazines also means that an advert may be viewed at a higher frequency than would be possible on TV. As one media planner put it: "You don't have to pay for repeat viewings in an issue of a women's magazine."

This image of comfort, credibility and privacy conveyed by women's magazines also explains the not infrequent attempts to make adverts look like editorial. An Anchor butter campaign, for instance, used TV advertising for "initial brand impact" and then followed this with a series of more comprehensive press adverts in women's magazines giving readers information about the "goodness" of butter. This in turn was supplemented by a poster campaign "to remind the housewife about the benefits of Anchor just before she does her shopping". As a Saatchi and Saatchi spokesman put it, quoted in the trade press: "We want the housewife to be absolutely certain that Anchor is the name she can rely on for real butter goodness, and we are confident that in the relaxed, intimate environment of women's magazines our conviction." (*Campaign*, 26 October, 1979)

Women's magazines are also favoured by media buyers for advertising domestic goods; it's recognised, not surprisingly, that women make eighty per cent of domestic purchasing decisions, a statistic which has hardly changed since the 1930s. It's important to point out, however, that the term "housewife" does not mean women stuck at home. It describes the person who makes the decisions about "which brand of loo paper or butter to buy". It therefore embraces all the women who fulfil a dual function and go out to work, *and* the estimated five per cent of men who as bachelors or family shoppers make the purchasing decisions. In recent years this percentage is thought to have increased, and some TV ads have appeared clearly addressing the sale of domestic/ food products to men.

Media planning's involvement with the initial creative strategy is complemented by follow-up market research to find out whether or not the mix has worked. Although it is difficult to assess the immediate impact of a campaign – whether or not people are actually starting to buy/increasing their purchases of a branded good – it is possible through quantitative and qualitative research to assess audience response to an advert. BMP, for example, conducted on-going research throughout the GLC campaign not only to assess people's response to the ad concept *before* it was placed, but also the impact which the campaign had in changing people's opinion about the GLC. This kind of information is fed back into the marketing mix to determine not only what kind of adverts should be produced, but also where they should be placed.

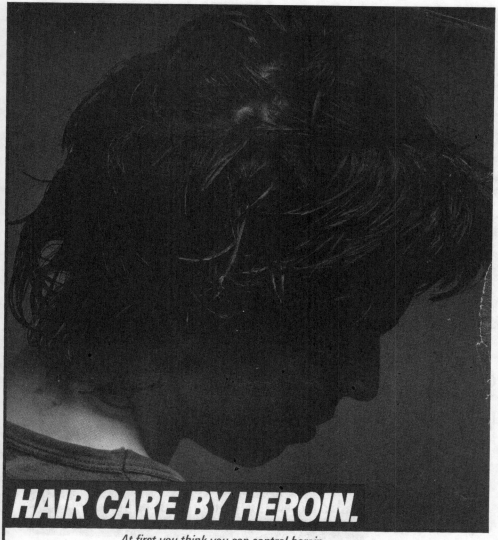

HAIR CARE BY HEROIN.

At first you think you can control heroin.

But before long you'll start looking ill, losing weight and feeling like death.

Then one day you'll wake up knowing that, instead of you controlling heroin, it now controls you.

So, if a friend offers you heroin, you know what to say.

HEROIN SCREWS YOU UP.

Tu. How to hold a conversation without saying a word.

All you need is Tu.
On your lips.
On your nails.
The shades are
honest. Extrovert. Never shy. 55p
for a lipstick. 55p for a nail colour.

The lip bite in Burn Up Rust.

Just stroke on
an exciting Tu lip
colour.

Moist lips in Rocking Red

Then match it with a glossy
Tu nail colour.
The rest is
up to you.
Others will get the message

The pout in Damned Pretty

and you needn't say a word.
Tu. The intimate you. The
seductive you.
It's a complete range of
highly coloured expression.
Fifteen matching
lip and nail colours in
plain and pearl that
say exactly
what is on your
mind.
Even if
you are too shy to say it
out loud.

15 Matching lip and nail Colours

tu

66

3

A CASE STUDY:
Selling cosmetics

1: The marketing problem

WOOLWORTHS USED TO be known as the "Sixpenny Store", thus named during the 1930s recession when the management boasted that nothing cost more than sixpence. This cheap, serviceable image had enabled the Woolworths empire to expand, sprouting a world-wide chain of stores stylistically reminiscent of contemporary picture palaces. The earlier Woolworths' stores, in cream facing with red lettering, still stand as a symbol of Depression Deco. But as the 1960s supermarket explosion transformed countless grocers into supergrocers, stocking everything from food to toiletries, cleaning equipment and haberdashery, Woolworths, still with key High Street sites, floundered under the weight of faulty management and falling sales. The empire had lost direction.

Woolworths was not quite a full range department store,

even less a competitive supermarket. Somehow the thrifty image became confused with cheapness, the store's "trusty" image rapidly replaced with one of shoddiness: the old people's shop where you could buy half a penn'orth of mints, a zip, a trowel and six matching tea towels. Woolworths' advertising, featuring lots of modern hi-tec goodies, did little to improve the public profile of the shop.

The most recent attempt to revitalise the flagging fortunes of Woolworths came when the company ditched its existing advertising agency, Allen, Brady and Marsh, in the summer of 1983. By January 1984, a new agency had been appointed: McCann Erickson, a company with considerable experience in retail trade advertising – it had just handled Tesco's "Check Out" campaign – and one of the first agencies in the 1950s to

Pictures opposite and overleaf:

TU cosmetics were launched by Woolworths to try to encourage more young women to come into the store. Used as a lure, they were strategically placed in the stores, encouraging women to browse and spend cash on other counters. The image chosen was of an ordinary girl in her twenties who could be glamourised by wearing TU. The creative brief specified: "Tu makes you the woman you would like to be - confident, attractive, modern."

Your eyes are the eyes of a little girl lost. Sort of helpless and don't know what to do.

All you need is Tu.

The range that puts a flashbang look in your eyes.

A glance will pin him to the wall.
Make him crawl.

Whispering shadows mix with wild colours in a frenzy of emotional hues.

3 LIKELY LASH.
3 LUSCIOUS LASHES.
12 PRECIOUS PEARLS AND 14 SHADES

Those eyes so helpless and appealing.

Eight Tu product ranges that let your eyes say what your lips would never dare. Fourteen plain and pearl Shades in single powder shadow packs and One Plain/One Pearl duo packs.

Super soft Stickers. Swivel eye shadow sticks for a subtle suggestion of colour.

And Kohl pencils to outline your intentions.

He'll get the message. And a page in your little black book.

One day will flash and send him crashing through the ceiling.

CREATED EXCLUSIVELY FOR WOOLWORTH

Tu. A little application can bring remarkable results.

With Tu only the slightest effort is required to put on a dazzling display.

Explore the endless possibilities our ranges offer and create a sensational result.

Match your lips and your fingertips with one of twenty-six glowing and vibrant colours. Feel free to establish your own co-ordinates. Luscious Lips provide an alternative route – with sponge-tip applicators and in eight ultra-glossy shades.

And if that's not exactly what you had in mind, there are always Smooth Talkers to turn to: four brilliant shades of lip gloss with which to put an end to the issue.

And that's it – you've completed the course.

With Tu you'll leave the competition standing.

CREATED EXCLUSIVELY FOR WOOLWORTH.

invest heavily in market research. This marketing experience resulted in a pitch for the Woolworths' account colloquially known as "Operation Tanner", a militaristic metaphor which harked back to the sixpenny image. The successful presentation to Woolworths included mock-up commercials plus a comprehensive dossier on Woolworths' marketing problems.

Exactly two years after the appointment of McCann's, Woolworths were once again to become restless. As *Campaign* magazine reported: "Woolworth is talking to agencies fuelling speculation that its £8.5m account, currently at McCann Erickson, is up for grabs. The client is said to have enjoyed a less than harmonious relationship with McCann in the past year." If the predecessor AMB (Allen, Brady and Marsh) had failed to appease Woolworths with its relentless "Wonder of Woolies" campaign, then McCann's contribution was described as "lacklustre".

This was not the first time that the company image had been overhauled. Woolworths' panic-stricken response to the recession of 1975/6 was not only to hire Allen, Brady and Marsh to handle all corporate image/product advertising, but to launch a new make up range. The agency given responsibility for this smaller account was NCK (Norman, Craig, Kummel). What happened to that campaign is the subject of this "case study".

*   *   *   *   *

"Tu" (as in the French for "you") was a make up range to be sold exclusively through Woolworths. One of the product's marketing missions would be to attract the younger woman into the store, which desperately needed the elixir of life as its clientele grew older. The advertising aim of NCK would therefore be to convince this younger woman that the range and, more importantly, Woolworths, was the place for her. As David Sinclair, the account executive for Tu emphasised: "Market research demonstrated that the majority of the store's customers were in the thirty to fifty age group, people who'd grown up using Woolworths. Younger women are important for a healthy retail trade, partly because they tend to have a higher disposable income than older women, and partly because Woolworths needs to create a new generation of brand loyal customers."

Woolworths had already noted the success of Boots (the Chemists) in this respect. Boots had promoted their own brand of cosmetics as a "hook" to the consumer, in the hope that once in the store they would buy other personal and domestic products. To accompany this strategy Boots had diversified their retail trade, moving away from a concentration on pharmaceutical and toiletry products and introducing health foods, records, electrical products, home appliances, etc. Cosmetics were similarly being introduced into supermarkets and Marks and Spencers for the same reason.

From the agency's point of view, these general marketing considerations had to be translated into a specific formula: a "problem" which strategic advertising could resolve. In terms of launching the cosmetic brand, two primary marketing considerations had to be analysed: a) the target market for the product; b) the position of the product on the market.

Target Market: The target market of the cosmetic brand necessarily had to reflect the wider marketing problems which Woolworths faced: namely, the need to encourage young women into the store. The market identified was therefore young women between the ages of nineteen and thirty, the "ball point", or focus, being women in their early twenties, the most desirable section of the young market. In economic terms, these women would be in the middle income bracket. The upper "AB" class were of less interest since they constituted only a small segment of the market which Woolworths wanted to solicit. Equally the lower income groups, the "DE"s, were rejected as financially unviable.

Product position: Woolworths already sold other established brands which appealed to the middle price range purchaser. Without exception all these brands tended to have a youthful consumer profile: for example, Rimmel, Outdoor Girl and Max Factor. The agency decided that Woolworths' own brand would be positioned against Max Factor, but more crucially, against Boots' own range of cosmetics. On one level this was to take trade away from the Boots' cosmetic ranges, but, more importantly, to try and establish Woolworths as a competitor to Boots in the retail trade. Max Factor and Boots' "7" and "17" already had established product identities. They were marketed as fashionable, colour co-ordinated comprehensive ranges. They appealed primarily to the kind of young woman who thought of herself as "sophisticated", "sexy" and "modern". Neither of these ranges were over-glamorous, they sold on the strength of "accessible", "believable" good looks. In order to compete, Tu would also need to be perceived as sexy and sophisticated.

Two further marketing considerations need to be borne in mind. The success of Boots' own ranges was reinforced by the tradition which the shop already enjoyed as "safe", "trusty", "scientifically approved". Woolworths felt they could not compete against this tradition of pharmaceutical reliability. Secondly, they would not compete on the strength of simply providing a comprehensive fashionable range of cosmetics, since both Boots and Max Factor had already established a leading style/fashion identity for their products.

2: The strategy

The image of Tu would therefore be "sexy and sophisticated"; and between 1978 and 1980, the interpretation of those words went through a series of creative crises and a succession of creative teams. The original approach had been to "capture mood". As a result, a series of "film noir" style enigmas were created. Shots of a girl's clothes cascading across a carpet towards a half open door. Presumably the bedroom. No pack shot, no model, no made up face. On reflection, though, this approach was probably *too* sophisticated. David Sinclair: "There were copy lines like 'Take off everything else but leave on Tu', which alluded to the woman having an affair. That kind of sensuality was probably a little too blatant, too upmarket for the young C1–C2 women we wanted." As a launch campaign, the earlier strategies were also fettered by the lack of "product". Sinclair felt that with a more established brand it might be possible to get away with

"image, mood and ambiance", but for an embryonic brand like Tu it was imperative to show the product range and, more importantly, its effect.

The creative breakthrough came in 1979 with the appointment of a new team and an overhauling of the advertising strategy. The "tone of voice" needed to be changed. The approach would be "intriguing, emotive and persuasive". Research into Tu's potential product position pointed to the uselessness of trying to compete against Boots' brand ranges (No.7 and 17) on the strength of product purity, skincare benefit, etc. The best alternative was to sell Tu on the strength of a glamorous image. But the creative problem confronting NCK was that while the young female consumer might like to perceive herself as sophisticated, research indicated that her actual knowledge of how to use cosmetics was limited. The image of sophistication needed to be tempered with education. So six "key elements" were selected for further elaboration. In practice, these uses applied equally well to a host of other similar products on the market, but the aims of successful image creation would be to make them appear unique to Tu.

TV product benefit:
1979 campaign
Tu: As a fashionable and comprehensive range of colour co-ordinated make

up which tied in with the seasonal changes in the fashion industry.

Tu: As a primarily youthful range aimed at the more "sophisticated girl".

Tu: A make up range capable of transforming the look of the face, creating a series of different make up effects.

Tu: As easy to apply.

Tu: As a reasonably priced product.

Tu: An exclusive range for Woolworths.

These creative priorities were interpreted in the resulting adverts which successfully relaunched Tu through a range of women's magazines, including *Cosmopolitan*. The creative team developed the theme of mood and sultry atmosphere, added face shots to show what the finished effect looked like, and ran copy which described the make up range. The new copy lines ran: "How to hold a conversation without saying a word" and "When you're too shy to say it, show it". The latter had a cute, waif-like peroxide blonde in a black dress peering coyly at the camera over her shoulder. The information aspect of the brief was incorporated into the body copy. Tu was billed as a comprehensive make up range: lipstick, nail colour, eye shadow etc. "Tu gleamers let your eyes say what your lips would never dare." The emphasis was on tame independence, make up to bring the young wallflower

out of hiding.

That campaign, and the equally successful follow-up, were thought to have boosted Tu sales by over fifty per cent. But whilst this latter campaign was judged commercially successful, it met with much dissension within NCK. The so-called "transformation" adverts showed the before and after Tu look. Headlines included: "For The Girl With a Colourless Past, A Colourful Future" and "Those Eyes So Helpless and Appealing, One Day Will Flash And Send Him Crashing Through The Ceiling." The message was that control over your make up meant control over your life and man. Other creative teams in NCK commented that the copy was too "clever, clever" and that it did little to break with the image that women made up their faces for men.

Several creative teams contested for the following year's (1980) campaign, the creative brief for which was a development of previous successes. David Sinclair described the aims of the 1980 campaign as the need "to project Tu as a comprehensive fashion range. Our new creative strategy is to depict highly attractive girls in what have been traditionally male situations. However, their good looks and femininity work to counter the masculinity of their environment". The resulting campaign was the product of a battle between copy writer and art director. The former pitched for a "more sexy look" than the previous campaign; the latter was sick of the "making up for men" emphasis of Tu and wanted something more independent. The result was a compromise, a series of "fantasy achievement" shots. They included a girl lounging languidly in the cockpit of a helicopter, another in ski gear, a third in a space helmet holding the original "moon camera".

The emphasis again was on image, "product benefit the consumer could experience", instead of simple branding. As the copy writer put it: "Make up is an image industry, the product is an illusion, a promise, not the brushes and applicators and creams that make it happen. Branding the name of Tu into every woman's mind might make them remember it, but it won't make them use it. It has to mean something to them. If you're talking about product benefit in the functional sense, then there's not a lot to recommend make up. All it does is clog up the skin. But psychological benefit is another thing. Make up makes women feel better. It's all fantasy, dreams which have a carry over into everyday life." In response to this philosophy the advert combined an element of surreal fantasy – "much better than production line or typing pool shots" – with vaguely educational body copy, including a list of Tu products. The new headline ran: "A little application can bring remarkable results".

Tu adverts subsequently appeared in a variety of women's magazines whose readership profile corresponded with the target market of nineteen to thirty year old women. These included *Honey* and *Cosmopolitan*.

3: The image

For David Sinclair in accounts the need to produce an aesthetically stylish advert sprang from different considerations. "Tu advertising needs to be different because there's so much bland and pretty cosmetic advertising around," he explains. "But the images we want aren't meant to be realistic, they incorporate an aspirational approach. We want to get across the point that changing your face is a step towards changing your life; so it's important to include an element of instruction – or the term we've come up with, application – to get the how across."

Sinclair felt that in the field of cosmetic advertising, the most important thing in setting "the tone" of the advert was to get the age group right. "Age is much more important than class in determining how people think and feel about their looks," he ascertained. For this reason the Tu creative brief clearly pointed to the "ballpoint" of the target market. Whilst Tu would be aimed at women between nineteen and thirty, the ballpoint – in terms of anticipated sales, and as a corollary the youthful look of the commercial – would be a woman in her early twenties.

The tyranny of age over other considerations in the selection of a target market for a cosmetic product was borne out by agency executives on other make up accounts. Grayham Giles pointed out that the Revlon account was stratified into seven different make up franchises, each designed to appeal to a different age group: Charlie was targeted at the older teenager; Ultima 2 at the older, more affluent woman; Princess Marcella Bougene a limited "status" brand, and so on.

Even so, most target markets are assessed by agencies on the strength of their lifestyle characteristics, as well as age. Agencies are often in disagreement about whether age, lifestyle, income or, indeed, the merits of the product, are the most important considerations in assessing purchasing patterns. David Sinclair, for example, was quite adamant that "the functional benefits outweigh the lifestyle aspect in the sale of a product." Carole Cootes, Ogilvy, Benson, Mather's research planner for Avon cosmetics, disagreed: "Most competing products on sale have similar functional benefits. It's very hard to sell a middle price

cosmetic range on the exclusive nature of its ingredients. A lot of 'image' advertising' falls into two camps. Either, as with Estée Lauder or Charlie, the company choose to select a look or face to represent their range; or they promote lifestyle. Our research indicates that women are very attentive to the clues of lifestyle in adverts."

Despite Sinclair's belief in the importance of age and product benefit as the determining factors, he reserved judgement over the sale of toiletries. "There is a real problem with fragrances. You can't talk about the specific product benefits. What exactly does a fragrance do, for example? You inevitably end up in the image market."

The prediction that lifestyle would become an indispensable marketing concept by the mid-1980s has come true. But whilst it is now central to agency thinking, it represents a very complex and at times confusing assessment of social status. As one account executive put it: "The difference between a traditional job or income defined notion of class, and the concept of lifestyle, is that the latter incorporates an element of aspiration."

The importance of aspiration in the lifestyle equation cannot be underestimated. As OMB's Carol Cootes put it: "Our potential market already knows that she's a suburban mum or housewife. She doesn't

Picture above:

Avon models are chosen for their "girl next door" look, so that women look at the adverts and think, "Yes, I could look like that too." "Charlie", the teen fragrance success of the 1970s, pushed the brand image a little further. The parent company Revlon replaced the soft girl next door concept with "the modern young girl of today. Independent and not needing a man, but still feminine, not into women's lib." The trousered tomboy was a sensation, pubescent teens up and down the country dreamed of better things than holding sweaty hands in the back of the cinema, and for a few summers at least the top decks of London buses reeked of Revlon's "gorgeous, sexy young fragrance".

The Magic of a Good Night's Sleep

You naturally want your family to enjoy a good night's rest every night. That's why you send them to bed with Horlicks.

As well as wise mother instinct this is sound medical sense. Children need nourishment for those long hours of sleep. That is why Horlicks is called the food-drink of the night. Another good thing—they love its taste.

Horlicks for you, yourself

For you, yourself, and for your husband and grown-up children, Horlicks at bedtime makes sound medical sense as well. Adults, after the stress and strain of working days, must have calm, regular sleep. Horlicks helps you relax into sleep—then go on sleeping. And wake with stored-up energy.

Horlicks, and only Horlicks, combines its creaminess with a calm digestibility to soothe you through the long night hours. Horlicks is no thin over-stimulating drink, no dulling drug. It is a natural food-drink with all the goodness of golden malted barley, creamy milk.

There's a whole new world of magic awaiting in regular sleep that many people never know. **Make sure in your family that Horlicks is always the bedtime drink.**

Picture above:

Facets of the 1960s. Lifestyle as luxury. The concept of lifestyle was to be elaborated to include people's aspirations and fantasies. Lifestyle didn't describe what you did. It described what you wanted to do. This image comes from Doctor's Orders, **a medical health publication. Horlicks used crude status symbols in its bid to associate the product with restful silk couches the size of cadillacs.**

need us to tell her that." So lifestyle is not a direct "reflection" of the way that people actually live their lives. It is not principled on "documentary" evidence. And it is on the subject of aspiration that agency staff are most defensive, waiting for the accusation that they "mislead" people, encourage false aims and ambitions, incite greed and promote sexual and racial stereotypes. The production of over glamourised images of women, for example, is often justified in terms of idealism. Over and again agencies will talk about people's needs for ideals, "what's wrong with a pretty girl" or "we're selling people the kind of fantasies

they want for themselves."

This soft soap dream selling is repackaged in terms of another advertising concept: personal benefit or product benefit the consumer can experience. This is short-hand for lifestyle aspiration. The fantasies that make people's lives livable. The emotions that justify a ten-hour shift on the shop floor. As a creative copy writer put it: "You're not selling somebody a car, you're selling them the reason why the car should be important to them. Making a space for it in their lives."

The key link between lifestyle and aspiration is "getting it right". Creative teams are often at pains to point out that "not any old fantasy will do."

The example of the mid-1970s' After Eight chocolate commercials illustrates the point. The TV commercial featuring a table full of "upper class nobs" eating After Eights doesn't mean that the chocolates are targeted at the lesser aristocracy. On the contrary, it's a humorous representation of how "working people" imagine the rich to live. A classic example of straightforward aspiration selling, little more advanced than the early Ponds cold cream ads in the 1930s which featured blue blooded models swathed in cream. If it's good enough for the toffs, it's good enough for . . .

Usually the problems facing aspirational selling are more complex than that. One of NCK's creative teams who worked on the Tu campaign also worked on the J. Weir jewellery account. The copy writer responsible said: "It's very important to get the nuances of lifestyle right. The J. Weir campaign was pitched at three different target markets. We called them the "sophisticated moderns", the "middle of the roads" and the "romantics." Each target group of women had pictures and copy doctored accordingly. A little more risqué for the "sophisticated moderns" who read *Company* and *Cosmopolitan*, moralistic and pure for down-market C2–Ds who read "romantic" magazines like *Annabel*, *True*, *Loving*, etc. In his mind the copy writer had a cameo of "the kind of woman" who would read each advert.

Lifestyle is not reducible, then, to a "classic" definition of class, which is solely income or occupation based. Income, as the evolution of the affluent worker illustrates, is no longer an indication of consumer tastes and preferences. As one account executive put it: "We're more interested in where people are going to than where they're coming from." This emphasis on consumption is what differentiates the NRS profile from, say, a classic Marxist class profile which positions people by virtue of their relationship to production or, rather, the ownership of the means of production. This shift from production based categorisation to a consumption based system is a trend in marketing and advertising which has evolved fluently from the 1930s onwards.

As we shall see later, this conceptual leap from production based thinking to consumption based thinking has provided much of the ammunition for schools of thought critical of advertising. The industry is often accused of "concealing" the true state of affairs. On the one hand "concealing" the "truth" of how goods are produced in an exploitative capitalist economy, and on the other, stimulating "false needs" and aspirations in the hearts and pockets of the public. It is on this issue that advertising logic frequently falls prey to inconsistency. As Mandate's account executive put it: "Mandate created a market, or rather perceived the need that was already there." Clearly, these two statements could be interpreted as contradictory. Creating a market (not already there) is part and parcel of a successful advertising function. Creating markets is dependent upon giving a product a brand identity which has appeal or meaning for a target market. By comparison, "a need that was already there" suggests that Mandate "found a gap", an unfulfilled pre-ordained desire in the mind of the prospective consumer. Target markets, like brand images, do not pre-exist advertising. People, like products, have identities forged for them. This, then, is one of advertising's primary functions: to make individuals behave in a predictable group fashion, that is, to buy the product in question.

As OBM's *Consumers' View of How Advertising Works* put it: "Defining the required responses from the consumer is the true expression of creative strategy", a feat only accomplished by "total immersion in the needs and lives of the target consumer. [Then] you will be able to conceptualise who they are and what they want. Only from that detail will come the insight and understanding you are seeking to make relevant and creative advertising."

Picture opposite:

Montage claims that the juxtaposition of unfamiliar or non-complementary elements is a way of opening up meanings, forging new connections and revealing the "true" conditions which underpin everyday appearances.

'We have a duty to protect the most vulnerable members of our society, many of whom contributed to the heritage we now enjoy.'

CONSERVATIVE MANIFESTO 1983

No F.T.....No Comment

4

THE BLACK MAGIC SYSTEM

ADVERTISING HAS NEVER had an easy ride. The political left and right have with equal venom cast aspersions on its practice and motivations. F. P. Bishop summed up his castigations in a "Threefold Charge": "Advertising represents business in its most aggressive relation to the consumer, in its attempts to influence the minds and desires of human beings and to impose on them its own scale of values... It is accused of misleading the public not merely as to the qualities of the goods they buy, but as to the whole range of motives and ideas by which their lives should be guided." And advertising is ultimately accused of replacing a social sense of purpose with "an acquisitive ideology in which the satisfaction of material desires is held up as the sole or principal end for the individual and the group." (*The Ethics of Advertising*, 1949)

This Christian outrage is remarkably similar in tone to the political criticism mounted by the broad left in Britain over the past twenty-five years. For example, advertising's lack of social responsibility is a major thrust of Gillian Dyer's socialist attack on advertising: "If we, the public, were offered a genuine choice of goods and services, then most of us would be perfectly capable of judging private consumption against other pressing priorities, like better health services and schools or more recreational facilities. But our economy is not geared towards the social services, and our real freedom of choice is by and large sacrificed to the flow of chocolates, shampoos, breakfast cereals and dog foods which gush out of factories." So the logic goes that if we were not seduced by the glamour and luxury of the advertising world, we would make "proper" rational decisions about what to consume.

But how does advertising achieve this invidious aim? The answer, put simply, is by magic. Most of the critics of advertising perceive the pro-

Picture opposite:

Full frontal subversion. Postcards obtainable from South Atlantic Souvenirs.

83

fession as sophisticated black magic, twentieth century Voodoo that appeals to our most base and animal desires for status, wealth and sex appeal. Advertising is the new demonology, the false god that despite ourselves we worship. Dyer puts forward the proposition that "the reason we have to be magically induced to buy things through fantasy situations and satisfactions is because advertisers cannot rely on rational argument to sell their goods in sufficient quantity."

Raymond Williams takes the point further, arguing for advertising's role in the destruction of a decadent society. "The skilled magicians, the masters of the masses, must be seen as ultimately involved in the meanings and values generally involved in the general weakness which they not only exploit but are exploited by." If society is on the verge of collapse, "then the magic system must come, mixing its charms and expedients with reality in easily available forms, and binding the weakness to the condition which has created it. Advertising is then no longer merely a way of selling goods, it is a true part of the culture of a confused society." (*Problems in Materialism and Culture*)

This demonology verges on possession. Like Dorian Grey, we sell our souls in the supermarket for the promise of eternal life, anti-wrinkle cream and fat-fighting foods. "Advertisements are selling us something else besides consumer goods: in providing us with a structure in which we, and those goods, are interchangeable, they are selling us ourselves." (Judith Williamson, *Decoding Advertisements*)

The key issue at stake in each of these gospels is that advertising perverts truth. On this, the left and the right are equally vociferous. The ASA (Advertising Standards Authority) and the IBA (spearheaded by the Honest, Decent, Legal and True campaign) may have within their mandate the protection of the public from false claims. Indeed, advertising is one of the most heavily proscribed industries – netted, hemmed in and overshadowed by the fear of inaccuracy or "misleading the public". But critics of advertising regard self-regulatory bodies such as the IBA or ASA as emasculated organisations upholding the status quo. And there is ample evidence to support this. The ASA, for example, has been slow to back feminists against sexist advertising, and the IBA has repeatedly endorsed reactionary policies, for instance refusing to transmit contraceptive or sanitary protection commercials likely to offend a "family audience".

The truth in question though is not about misleading facts, but about the quality of life promoted by the advertising system. Advertising's major crime, it is argued, is that it conceals the "true" condition of life, true needs and social wants, replacing them with a glamorous and ultimately inaccessible fantasy world. It is a dream factory, promoting the dreams of the powerful and the rich at the expense of the disenfranchised and poor. Advertising's dream is an act of pernicious ideology: like Orwell's *1984*, advertising promotes a false vision of life as a method of social control. "Advertising appropriates things from the real world, from society and history and sets them to its own work. In doing so it mystifies the real world and deprives us of any understanding of it. We are invited to live an unreal life through the ads." (Gillian Dyer)

But whilst the bible-bashing rhetoric which inflamed the moralists might appear similar to contemporary cultural criticism, the rationale behind it is different. The ethical argument takes to task the quality and kind of good produced by industry, the method of selling and the motivation of the consumer in desiring the acquisition of status symbols and luxury goods. This protestant zeal is primarily concerned with the display, not the possession of private wealth. Ethical/moral arguments are therefore fundamentally conservative. They wish to maintain the status quo, value tradition and the power relations which already govern society.

By comparison, the left political objections to advertising see it as only the tip of a corrupt iceberg. Advertising is the PR profession for capitalism, justifying rampant consumerism, diverting resources away from the economic infrastructure and reinforcing the values which perpetuate inequality and economic exploitation. In short, advertising is part of capitalism's self-justification system, its ideology.

The feminist response

Ever since the birth of advertising, the political left has therefore been attempting to undermine its potency, to show what the world is "really" like. But it is only in these more recent periods that these objections have been formulated into active strategies. At the forefront of these campaigns have been those concerned about representations of women.

Advertising is seen as reinforcing a particularly repressive aspect of ideology: whilst women pioneer for better opportunities in the "real" world, the media continues to churn out out-moded images of womanhood. Despite the many contemporary advertising commercials which play on women's independence – their ability to make up their own

Pictures on next pages:

Jill Posner, Direct Response advertising. Some of the best examples of feminist graffiti now marketed as a guerrilla art form. Postcards obtainable from The Women's Press, 124 Shoreditch High Street, London E1 6JE, 01-729-5257.

mind in the consumer jungle – it is still true that most adverts continue to define women as housewives, reflecting limited roles and images of work and leisure. This continued mismatch between the world of the advertising image and the real world of "the second sex" precipitated the feminist outrage of the late 1960s and 1970s.

Books like *Is This Your Life?* by Josephine King and Mary Stott (Virago, 1977) and *The Gender Trap: Messages and Images* by Carol Adams and Rae Laurikietis (Virago, 1976) provided, as part of their consciousness-raising, direct comparisons between the stereotyped world of advertising and real life. *The Gender Trap*, for example, isolated five dominant stereotypes in the media: The Carefree Girl, The Career Woman, The Hostess, The Wife and Mother and, finally, The Model. Criticism focused on the ways in which these idealised, glamourised images damaged and manipulated women, making them feel second class citizens – fat, lumpy, wrinkled and unlovable. The media was condemned for promoting anorexia in girls, inciting ultra slimness, "Twiggy" limbs and unhealthy self-images.

In *The Gender Trap* the gulf between fact and fantasy is nowhere more apparent than in the role of The Model: "She bears the least resemblance to real life. For the most part she advertises clothes and make up. She's cool, distant and untouchable. The background will always be an exotic, unusual, perhaps slightly fantastical one. She'll never be seen putting out the milk or fetching in the coal. As a beautiful object she is on show all the time and will never let herself down." Feminism effectively accused advertising and the media of producing not only misleading, but also dangerously subversive images of women, crushing them into insecurity, a man's arms and the kitchen sink.

Women's response to the media's resistance to change, and belligerence in the face of "hysterical hairy dykes", was to gather steam and evolve a range of tactics. The concern which inspired books like Ann Oakley's *Housewife*, Germaine Greer's *The Female Eunuch* and Shulamith Firestone's *Dialectics of Sex*, spilled over into direct action. Feminist campaigns included the defacing and re-captioning of posters and hoardings in the street and on public transport. Campaign groups started to produce anti-sexist stickers to place on offending adverts in public spaces. Spray guns came out, producing a spate of creative alternative grafitti. Pictures of bare breasts were rubbed out, blacked out or covered up.

By the early 1980s the movement had gathered such steam that even Soho, the sanctuary of sin and sex, was under assault as women began successfully to "reclaim the night". Emasculated punters grabbed their brown paper bags, macs and flies and rushed for the nearest exit. Blue movies, sex shops, porno newsagents, were all picketed with equal enthusiasm. Women slept out on the streets and films like *Not A Love Story* depicted scenes of women haranguing men in peep shows about their intentions and inhibitions.

Groups such as WAVAW (Women Against Violence Against Women) saw pornography and advertising as different ends of the same spectrum: images produced by a misogynist patriarchy to endanger the lives of the female species. Adverts like "Underneath they're all lovable" (the much quoted "rape inspiring" Lovable bra advert which added impetus to the feminist cause) were seen as offensive not by virtue of explicitness but because they degraded women, reducing them to the status of objects. The most extreme wings of feminism claimed that they actually encouraged rape and sexual assault. The sexist image had suddenly become much more than offensive and misleading, it was actually inciting men to commit crimes against women.

The idea that an image could produce action was, ironically, precisely what the advertising industry had been trying to convince its clients of for the past century. Successful advertising could produce sales, and so, the argument went, the successful selling of women as a commodity could produce rape. In a perverted way violent sex was the "benefit the consumer could experience" and women the branded good.

The most extreme reaction was censorship. Not only were sections of the feminist movement picketing and daubing offensive images, they were also suggesting that the process of education be halted in favour of protectionism. It was wrong that women should be forced to see pictures of their exploited sisters. The nude should under all conditions – except in the most sacred and obscure feminist medical journals – be excluded. Men, it appeared, would take any opportunity to slaver over the limbs of a naked female. It was prohibition all over again.

Meanwhile, the New Right had adopted similar tactics. Led by Mary Whitehouse, the Festival of Light and the reactionary Viewers' and Listeners' Association were busy petitioning the government, Smiths newsagents and the press to ban "offensive" images from our screens and streets. Whilst the feminist cause was women, The Light fought for The Family, at that time organised around the moral panic of video nasties – those soul snatchers on celluloid that invaded the lounge and made off with the minds of the under fives. But the White

Light argument was essentially identical to the radical feminists'. Pictures have the power to pervert. Offensive images don't make you just think dangerous thoughts, they make you do dastardly deeds.

Other sections of the libertarian left were more confused in their response, wary of condoning censorship. This form of State control could easily backlash, resulting in the policing of left and alternative publications. Many feminists feared that the small print of the Video Recordings Bill, for example, could affect the publication of such "explicit" health books as *Our Bodies Ourselves* and even that hallowed feminist organ, *Spare Rib*.

Altered images: photography and photomontage

Another approach to the issue was to subvert the impact of the media, and advertising in particular, through the production of so-called "positive" images. Taking as the starting point a faith in the camera's ability to reproduce "real life", producing positive images meant getting away from the false world of the media; it meant portraying women in "positive" ways. This ranged from simple photographs of girls having fun, to pictures of women at Greenham Com-

mon fighting for a cause, to the "truck driver" syndrome. The latter meant depicting women in unfamiliar roles – carpenter, lorry driver, printer – usually reproduced in magazines like *Spare Rib* and *Camerawork*.

This concern to record the real conditions of working lives usually ignored or glamourised in advertising and the media has an honourable heritage in the "worker photography" movement, whose history is worth briefly recalling.

Worker photography was not in fact intentionally conceived as an assault on the fantasy world of the media. If anything it owes its origin to the early "social comment" documentary photography produced by the Mass Observation project. This was not a worker inspiration but sprung from the philanthropy of 1930s liberals and socialists: "The [motivations] ranged from guilt born of a sense of privilege to the excitement (including for some, the aesthetic stimulation), of exploring unknown country; from the desire just to have a good time to an impulse to help make the world better by seeking out and disseminating the facts about other people's lives." (Jeremy Mulford: Introduction to Humphrey Spender's *Worktown People*).

The pictures produced by the Mass Observation team have often been accused of being "candid camera" snaps of the working classes at play and recreation. The tyranny of

Ashtrays and the extensive dirty floors of the airport.
The arrivals and departure board of Heathrow and the overalls from Acme.
A glimpse of exploitation on your way to New York.

IMMIGRANT-LABOUR

Rajput windows and the ethereal voice of the sitar.
Murals of the legends of Krishna and silks and brocades from Rajasthan.
A glimpse of India on your way to New York.

AIR-INDIA

a relation between THINGS

Who's holding more than the baby?

Being a mother and a housewife not only
means having kids and looking after them,
so that one day they can be workers.
It also means keeping men clean and fed
and emotionally supported - in other words
keeping them in working order, fit for the
factory or the office or the dole queue.
This maintenance work is unpaid and under-
valued. If all women went on strike, our
society would grind to a halt.

Images of Correction: During the mid 70s many political artists
were concerned with the ideological message of advertising. This
'misleading' information was commented upon through the
devises of montage, simulation and juxtapostion. In different
ways the work of The Hackney Flashers, Yve Lomax and Paul
Wombell sought to correct the world represented in the advert.
The cleaning staff of Air India, the domestic cooker or the kitchen
scene all refer to an aspect of women's sexual identity and labour
which is absent in the advertisement. In this sense these images
of correction referred to a reality which was thought to exist
outside the image.

30

the snooping camera, even in such a worthy Dickensian "social rights" cause, meant that many of the photographers had reservations about taking shots of interiors, prying too much into poverty-stricken lives. This philanthropic ambition of photography still finds amplification today in the charity photographs produced for Oxfam. Such photographs rest on the critical edge between highlighting the atrocities of poverty and attempting to restore dignity to the notion of a working class community.

In principle at least, this was a dilemma easily resolved by taking the cameras out of the hands of concerned observers and handing them over to real working class people. In Germany during the 1930s, workers were called upon by the communist *AIZ* magazine to act as documentary reporters, photographing the struggle, the campaigning socialist spirit and the appalling work and home conditions of everyday life. Similar courses and projects were launched in America, Holland and Britain.

The German movement was under no illusions as to why workers initially contributed. Erich Rinka, general secretary of the Association of Worker Photographers of Germany, was quoted as saying: "Let us be quite clear, most workers with photographic interests did not come to us with the intention of fighting with their cameras; they came to prac-tise photography to learn technique. This is why we had to lead them to class consciousness photography above and beyond the technique and practice of the medium." (*Creative Camera*, No. 197/8)

The worker photography movement ultimately petered out, but its image and intention lived on through such popular publications as the illustrated *Picture Post* and, more recently, the "community photography" movement. Community photography has been described in *Camerawork*, a magazine which throughout the 1970s acted as a mouthpiece for the movement, as "concerned with the needs and preferences of local people. It aims to provide a resource in the form of photographic equipment, darkrooms and teaching or access to a photographer's services... Community work is essentially an educational process, bringing people together to achieve an immediate aim." But it's also clear that whilst a critique of capital's methods and message was implicit in the early documentary and worker photography, the community photography of the late 1970s and early 1980s demanded that this critique be made explicit.

This deliberate undermining of advertising's dream world was expressed during the 1970s in the work of photographers like Jo Spence and The Hackney Flashers. The device of simple juxtaposition

"You've tucked the kids into bed . . .
slipped into something simple. . .
taken your Valium. . .
and you're waiting for him to come home. . .

mustn't be late for the evening shift at the
bread factory".

Cutex

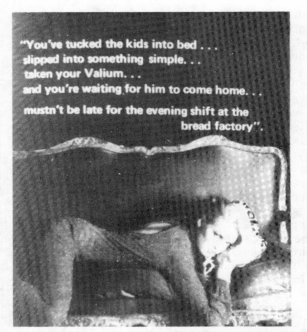

look sewn up. And summed up.

Main picture: Her long skirt and gilet in look pink 'Crimplene'. Small, medium or large. £81.00.

Centrepicture: Her long skirt and tube-top in red or black 'Crimplene.' Small or medium. £57.00. His two-piece suit in black or navy pure cotton velvet. From 'Trend' department. £95.00.

Far left: Her gilet coat in navy/white check and toning skirt in navy/white stripe. Both in wool. Worn with shirt in white viscose. All small, medium or large. £99.50 for the three pieces. His navy cotton corduroy jacket, grey wool trousers and three-piece suit from 'Trend' department. £125.00.

MERRY XMAS?

For these children and many others, this Xmas will be a time of particular hardship – together we can help. Special toy collection centres are now open at Clydvan centre – Bleangwynfi (0639) 851285. Youth Centre – Glyncorrwg (0639) 851485. Nantyfyllon Institute – Maesteg (0656) 732218.

Fight for the Future of your Children
KEEP MINING IN MAESTEG
If you can offer food, toys, or money to help local miners and their families this winter – please contact: Nantyfyllon Institute, Bangor Terrace, Maesteg. Tel: Maesteg 732218/739151. Cheques/postal orders can be made payable to the 'Maesteg Contingency Fund' – TSB Acc. no. 084 87450 Bank code no. 77-65-18

Left:
Victim photography? Like the Oxfam poster, socially committed photography geared to expose the exploitation of the people, can unwittingly expose too much. Heart-string images with their quivering humanity hover on the divide between protector and persecutor.

Hackney Flashers:
Feminist photography of the 1970s used the techniques of montage and juxtaposition to make simple, lucid statements about women's exploited position in the labour force. This technique was perhaps most effective when they turned their attention, and their lenses, to the subversion of advertising. The slippery brittleness of a nail polish advert is cracked and made redundant by reference to what women do with their hands all day. Taken from Photography/Politics 1.

(Photography/Politics 2, also published by Comedia, will be available in Autumn, 1986.)

95

of the false and the real was used over and again. Paul Wombell's 1975 "Air India – Immigrant Labour" image, for example, compared a lush Air India advert featuring a beautiful air hostess with a photograph of an Indian woman cleaning the airport lounge. The original Air India caption read: "Rajput windows and the ethereal voice of the sitar. Murals of the legends of Krishna and silks and brocades from Rajasthan. A glimpse of India on your way to New York." This was cleverly subverted by Wombell's alternative "Ash trays and extensive dirty floors of the airport. The arrivals and departure board of Heathrow and the overalls from Acme. A glimpse of exploitation on your way to New York." Similarly, the compilations of Yve Lomax and The Hackney Flashers juxtaposed glamourised images of women with kitchen sink reality.

This use of juxtaposition revealed a fundamental concern for alternative photographers. The documentary image in isolation was inadequate. Pictures of women working, men down the pits or dole queues, could give an impression of what "real" life was like, but they could not make a political statement. Impressions of poverty could be used as much against the working people as for them. The Tory press, for example, had for generations used similar photographs (dole queues, dirty kitchens, men on street corners) to illustrate how lazy and inept the working classes were. Ironically, the documentary style of photography could betray the cause.

The limitations of documentary photography were recognised, in fact, right from the start of the worker photography movement. As in the simple juxtapositions of modern artists like Wombell and Lomax, photomontage – the appliqué of images from different sources – was used to undermine the dominant ideology through the "making up" of photographs. Of course, advertising also uses photomontage seamlessly to combine elements from different sources in such a way as to make their marriage look natural (for example, in the White Horse whisky commercials). Here the airbrush, computer paintbox, retouching and reshooting work to suspend reality, weaving a fanciful web of fiction, reinforcing and glamourising the brand name/image of a product. Political photomontage, on the other hand, attempts to reverse the process, so that the juxtaposition of unfamiliar or non-complementary elements is a way of opening up meanings, and revealing the "true" conditions which underpin everyday appearances.

John Heartfield, one of the earliest and best known photomontagists, produced such effective anti-Nazi propaganda, printed in magazines like the

Communist *AIZ*, that in the early 1930s he was forced to flee Germany, taking refuge in France and, finally, London. The device of the familiar reorganised into the extraordinary can be seen throughout Heartfield's work: Hitler's connection with big business is illustrated in the famous "Kleiner Mann bittet um grosse Gaben", where Hitler receives a backhander from banking magnates, whilst "Adolf the Superman Swallows Gold and Spouts Junk" features a supposed X-Ray of the Führer with his spine and internal organs replaced by gold coins.

The legacy of Heartfield's contribution to political propaganda can still be registered, influencing the work of contemporary political artists like Peter Kennard, Peter Dunn and Lorraine Leeson, who produced "Passing The Buck". This poster criticising the profits of international drug companies, and made for the East London Health Project and Hackney Trades Council, bears more than a passing resemblance in theme and execution to the Heartfield Hitler backhander. Victor Burgin has also used photomontage to criticise advertising, for instance in a poster which took a romantic advert of a couple and captioned it with a new text: "What Does Possession Mean To You? 7% of our population own 84% of our wealth."

In recent years, then, photomontage has been used as a visual game to play on and highlight the hypocrisies of advertising. Two fundamental assumptions underpin this. First, that the "natural" power of the camera to capture "real life" in the documentary shot is limited. Secondly, that a "fictional" image such as a montage is more capable of detecting the "truth" in a situation. Once this second point is accepted – that fiction may have greater political clout than descriptive documentary photography – it seriously weakens much of the left's traditional assault on the media and advertising. As Victor Burgin succinctly argues, advertising cannot be trashed simply on the strength of its manipulative, persuasive method: "Work with an obvious ideological slant is often condemned as 'manipulative'; that is to say, first that the photographer manipulates what comes over in the image; second, that as a result his or her audience's beliefs about the world are manipulated. Not much is known about how the media influences opinions, although we can be fairly sure that people aren't simply led by the nose by photographs. Whatever the case, both charges can be similarly answered: manipulation is of the essence of photography; photography would not exist without it." (*Camerawork*, no.3.)

Semiology: inside the fantasy factory

If advertising could not be criticised for telling blatant lies and falsehoods, then it meant that the left's critique of advertising needed to become more sophisticated. The idea that all messages are effectively constructed, and that all meaning is man-made, is essential to that branch of analysis called semiology.

Just as "lifestyle" was imported by the advertising industry from the States in the 1950s as a way of explaining the link between class and aspiration, so the left academics of the 1960s rejected the concept of aspiration in favour of "ideology" – that cluttered system of beliefs and corporate fantasies which masquerades as commonsense. Semiology, essentially a branch of linguistics, was imported from France because of its potential for unpicking the threads of ideology. The radicalising of language took on the air of a military manoeuvre. Semiology would enable the academic intelligence unit to "decode" the messages of capitalism. Herein lay the potential for change.

Under the academic wing of Althusser, ideology became an all-embracing value system from which there was no escape. What Marx had done for the Labour theory of value and class exploitation, Althusser promised to do for ideology. Ideology, according to Althusser, subsumed all of democracy's information systems: the media, education, art and the welfare state were all supporting and, worse still initiating, ideologies which deadened the soul, brainwashed the mind, and made revolution a decade further away. A post-industrial affluent gloom spread over academia.

Revolutionising the means of production was therefore no longer a guarantee that people would fight for freedom. Their aspirations had been filled with dishwashers, three door garages and blue movies. The corrupted soul of the worker had little to fight with; in the process of salvation the recuperation of the mind must be a first step to revolution. The media, and especially that spinner of affluent fantasies – advertising – had become the enemy. The battle over ideology was on.

The terrible truth was that advertising was in some grotesque sense "real". People saw adverts and bought twin-tubs. They watched glamorous movie stars and had their hair styled accordingly. Men married girls who looked like Monroe or Twiggy. Despite feminism, women on the whole wanted little more than two up, two down and two point four in the playpen. These "imaginary" perceptions were also capable of having "real" effects on the economy.

... besser als vom Storch gebissen!

The net result of these academic debates was to centralise advertising as the culprit. Whilst the media as an institution was blamed for reactionary ideologies, advertising – neatly pivoted between the act of producing and consuming a commodity – justified the whole capitalist system. In the introduction to *Decoding Advertisements* (1978), probably the most influential left critique of advertising produced during the 1970s, Judith Williamson said of the affluent worker: "Thus instead of being identified by what they produce, people are made to identify themselves with what they consume. From this arises the false assumption that workers with two cars and a colour TV are not part of the working class... The fundamental differences in our society are still class differences, but use of manufactured goods as a means of creating classes or groups forms an overlay on them."

Demonology and possession in advertising had been replaced by self-destructive vampirism. The worship of consumerism demanded the incessant consumption of more goods in order to survive. The theory fitted neatly: whilst capitalism sucked the worker dry through exploitation, the worker staved off the inevitable, cap tooth fangs sunk into fattening cakes, lush department stores, HP and drive-in DIY. The act of consuming enables us to consume ourselves: "We are both product and consumer; we consume, buy the product, yet we are the product. Thus our lives become our own creations, through buying; an identikit of different images of ourselves, created by different products." (Judith Williamson) The solution was to threaten the vampire with daylight. The methods of ideology would be exposed. And the silver cross had the word "semiology" printed on the hilt.

The basic question underpinning semiological analysis is how meaning is created. This question applies equally well to the analysis of a text or an image, because the solution lies in the identification of "signifiers". As Gillian Dyer points out: "The meaning of an advertisement is not something there, statistically inside an ad, waiting to be revealed by a correct interpretation. What an ad means depends on how it operates, how signs and its ideological effect are organised internally (within the text) and externally (in relation to production, circulation and consumption and in relation to technological, economic, legal and social relations)." The advert is treated as concentrated ideology, reinforcing certain values at the expense of others. Individualism, affluence and beauty take priority over, for example, basic

Picture opposite:
The phallic implications of sexualised selling made clear. Cigars, tumescing shaving sticks and permanently erect penises become interchangeable in these images which slip between subversion and affirmation of sexual stereotyping.

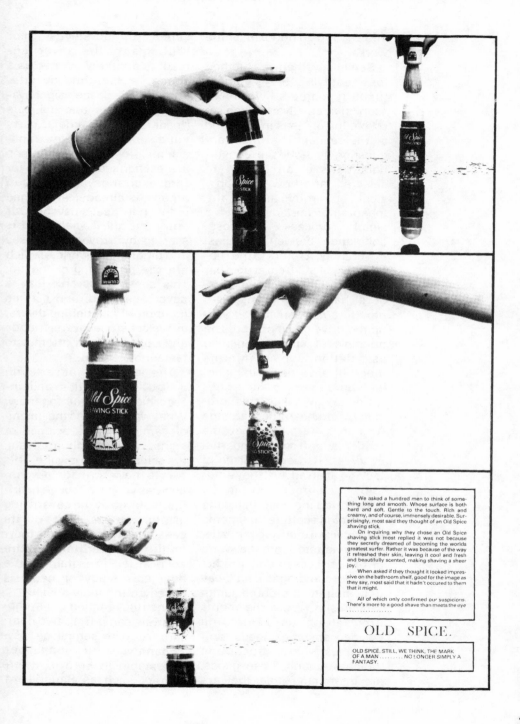

We asked a hundred men to think of something long and smooth. Whose surface is both hard and soft. Gentle to the touch. Rich and creamy, and of course, immensely desirable. Surprisingly, most said they thought of an Old Spice shaving stick.

On inquiring why they chose an Old Spice shaving stick most replied it was not because they secretly dreamed of becoming the worlds greatest surfer. Rather it was because of the way it refreshed their skin, leaving it cool and fresh and beautifully scented, making shaving a sheer joy.

When asked if they thought it looked impressive on the bathroom shelf, good for the image as they say, most said that it hadn't occured to them that it might.

All of which only confirmed our suspicions. There's more to a good shave than meets the eye . . . .

OLD SPICE.

OLD SPICE. STILL, WE THINK, THE MARK OF A MAN . . . . NO LONGER SIMPLY A FANTASY.

information on how a machine works.

Semiology, then, is a method for identifying the signifiers (usually objects, words or scenes) in an advert which set off chains of ideas in the mind of the reader. The important question is how the constituent parts of an image are selected, and how their physical proximity affects the meaning of the adverts. It's a simple process of cross-pollination between species. Put crudely, it refers to the rub-off effect of a 24-carat gold bar nestled up to a packet of fags, or a handsome young man next to a car parked half-way up the drive to a mansion. The principle of upwardly mobile association, which informs much of advertising thinking, isn't hard to grasp.

Semiology takes this process of orchestration a stage further by arguing that the reader is far from an impartial observer. Rather, by virtue of looking at an advert, they enter into a contract with it. By completing the meaning of the associated scattered elements (rather like a crossword puzzle) they've entered into the world of the advertisement. The act of understanding it is half way to buying it. To requote Judith Williamson: "Advertisements are selling us something beside consumer goods: providing us with a structure in which we, and those goods, are interchangeable, they are selling us ourselves." For Williamson, the advertisement is primarily defined as a space, a location or site. Within this space, sign systems, products and subjects (readers) meet in order to carry out a series of complex transactions, in which meanings are exchanged. The basis for this exchange, Williamson argues, is already established in the individual's psyche. Our entry into the social world is scarred by irrevocable losses and emotional wounds, which are the price of growing up. This sense of psychic loss is never alleviated, and acts as the motor force behind desire, as we consume lovers, friends and objects in an attempt to feel whole again.

The idea that advertising played on anxieties and insecurities was nothing new. What was new was the linking of semiology, the science of signs, with psychoanalysis, the science of the psyche. This was a new turn for psychoanalysis which, although heartily employed by the advertising profession as part of its consumer research, was thoroughly discredited by the political left in Britain as the bourgeois study of neurosis based on the individual.

The rejuvenation of psychoanalysis came from two quarters. As with semiology, psychoanalysis had long been acceptable in France, where writers such as Baudrilliard,

Althusser, Deleuze and Lacan had incorporated the theory of the psychic structure of the individual into their analysis of the motor force and power of capitalism. In Britain it was left to the intellectual wing of the feminist movement to reassess the potential of psychoanalysis. Magazines like *Screen*, *MF*, *Feminist Review*, and conferences like the 1976 Patriarchy Conference were all arguing the case for psychoanalysis, displaying its capacity to elucidate how women were marginalised from male culture, reared as second class citizens and effectively disenfranchised from personal power. On the basis of "the personal is political", psychoanalysis, together with semiology, had the capacity to show how ideology operated in and through the individual.

It is no accident that the political theory of the mid-1970s should have moved so far away from "crude economic determinism". From the feminist point of view, the fascination with ideology was twofold: partly because it helped explain people's resistance to change, and partly because ideology provided a framework with which to think through women's position not as producers, but as consumers. Women, after all, were the people to whom the image industry addressed itself. Women were the people who made eighty per cent of domestic purchasing decisions. Women were the people who actually went out and bought the commodity bricks which built up the lifestyle.

The theoretical breakthrough came when the feminist movement argued that women's obsession with the fruits of capitalism – shopping, family rearing, personal adornment – was not a result of inherent narcissism, nor "false consciousness" which made them blind to the "real" economic issues at stake. Rather, from the day they are born, women are constructed into their consumerist role. "For women, it was no longer possible to hold to simplistic views of ideology as 'false consciousness' or an inverted image of real relations. What was encountered... was the fact that women were constructed in those socio-familial relations of capitalism; their desires and needs were the desires and needs of those relations, not some distorted form of the true subject of needs which underlies the notion of alienation." (Coward Lipshitz, Cowie, *Psychoanalysis and Patriarchal Structures*, 1976)

It can be seen that in this work on ideology and the position of women in/outside the labour force, are the seeds for thinking through a theory of why and how people consume. In short, for developing a theory of consumption which would complement existing theories of production. At the moment such a theory does not exist. Quite simply, this is because consumption is not recognised as economically important. It always takes second place to theories of industry, levels of production, state intervention and inflation. When consumption is discussed, it is usually in sociological terms. The left calls it ideology, the economists call it tastes and preferences and advertising calls it lifestyles.

*   *   *   *   *   *

Most of the criticisms mounted on advertising by the political left have therefore been ideological criticisms: taking to task the images produced and the effects which these are likely to have on people's aspirations, identities and self-image. Feminist criticism of economic's inability to explain women's social position has been paralleled by a marked resistance amongst left economists to take advertising and marketing seriously; so much so that the words "advertising", "marketing" and "consumption" will rarely be found in the index of a traditional Marxist economics text.

And if the criticism thrust at advertising relies on the assumption that it appeals to the emotions, and not logic, and is

therefore underhand, the solution has been to "counterbalance" this with a supply of information. But whilst it has been part of the education service provided by the left to use *information* as a way of "revealing" the iniquities perpetrated by advertising, it does not follow that appealing to the *emotions* is inherently bad or subversive. The logical extension of this argument – waged in various forms from the Russian Revolution onward – is that art is out and only the computer print-out can be trusted.

It is worth repeating the point made by Victor Burgin earlier: "Manipulation is of the essence of photography; photography would not exist without it." It is also worth adding a later statement about semiology's capacity to "decode" the rhetoric of advertising: "The rhetorical structures of advertising are 'indifferent' to the emotional and ideological value of the contents they handle... there is no reason why, once the devices of advertising have been isolated by semiotic analysis, they may not be recycled in counter-ideological message making." (*Camerawork*, no.3) The point being made is twofold. First that the rhetoric of advertising can be used against itself but, more importantly, that the essentially fictional devices employed by advertising are

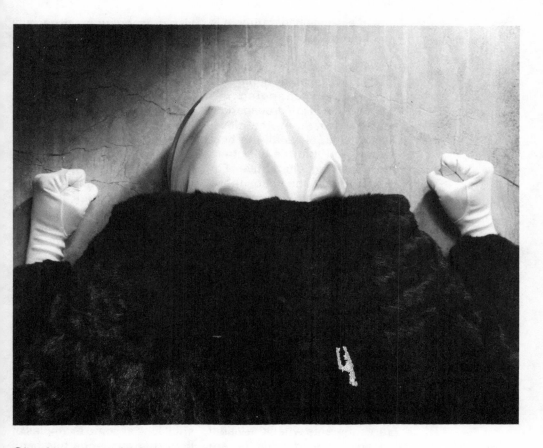

She began a glorious career
as an officer,
advanced to the highest positions,
showed herself superior
to all the men.
A man appeared at last
who surpassed
not only all men
but also surpassed her;
she subjected
herself to him,
yet with the most extreme anger.

not in essence bad: rather, it is the kind of fictions conveyed.

The feeling that the left is in some sense aesthetically and politically lagging behind is undoubtedly changing the complexion of left propaganda. It is a fear that the devil, advertising, plays all the best tunes, and that the left offers no appealing alternative. For underpinning the notion that a socialist system would represent and reproduce "real" needs, and rely on information as opposed to persuasion, is the knowledge that emotion is a powerful weapon in changing the hearts and minds of people. It is the fear that, underneath the gloss, the communication skills of advertising have to be admired, if not emulated.

This crisis in socialist perspective is poignantly illustrated in Robert Golden's observation of left culture: "In rare moments when the visual means of communication are given some attention we encounter a reliance upon old visual techniques, especially socialist realist and photomontage methods of the 1920s and 1930s, and advertising styles of the 1950s. This implies a cultural conservatism which is out of step with progressive political views... In order to communicate an idea which is by and large not consciously understood by working class people, yet an explanation of their lives, we must rely upon a visual vocabulary and style which is recognisable, knowing and entertaining. We are therefore immediately reliant to a degree on the methods of advertising if we are to attract people's eyes away from the seduction of the snappy competition we face. Our work must be as good or better than the competition selling cigarettes." (Robert Golden: *Photography and Politics One*, 1979) In the next chapter we shall look at some examples of how that challenge has been taken up.

Picture opposite:

Part of the front line of propaganda subversion, mixing advertising, montage and graphic styles in their war against Thatcherism and the state. Humour and hard-edged politics in a rare combination. Leeds Postcards can be obtained from PO Box 84, Leeds LS3 1AZ.

New Master PCR

5

SYMPATHY FOR THE DEVIL: SELLING POLITICS

FROM THE PRESIDENTIAL candidacy of Dwight Eisenhower in 1952, through to the marketing of Thatcher by Saatchi and Saatchi in 1983, commercial promotion has been a feature of transatlantic politics. And, traditionally, the British left's response to this has been negative. Labour ex-General Secretary Jim Mortimer commented on Thatcher's election victory in 1983: "I can assure you that the Labour Party will never follow such a line of presentation in politics, for very serious reasons. The welfare of human beings, the care of people and the need to overcome unemployment: these are the real tasks before us, not presenting people as if they're breakfast food or baked beans."

The difference now in Labour Party thinking over such controversial topics is apparent when Nick Grant, the ex-head of Party advertising could say, two years later: "The easy poke that we're not going to sell Labour like we sell soap powder, quite frankly doesn't gell anymore. It's so old fashioned to assume that advertising and opinion research has nothing to do with communicating with voters."

This chapter, then, is about how much the left's attitude to using advertising and marketing has changed over the past few years. To illustrate this I have taken three examples of left institutions and enterprises which have faced the advertising issue head on – the Greater London Council, the Labour Party and *City Limits* magazine.

1: The Greater London Council

The advertising campaign for the Greater London Council was, without doubt, the most successful in "left" history. It was also adjudged successful by the industry, scooping most of the major advertising awards. Equally successful in shifting public opinion, the campaign

Picture opposite:

Competing campaigns; facets of Labour and Conservative pre-election TV campaign work from 1983. As early as the 1950s, Dwight Eisenhower had predicted that future elections would be fought on TV, not on the streets. (Pictures by Neil Martenson).

IF YOU HAVE ANY COMPLAINTS WHEN THE GLC GOES, YOU'LL BE TALKING TO WHITEHALL.

SAY NO TO NO SAY.

FROM NOW ON YOU HAVE NO SAY IN WHO RUNS LONDON.

Did you know Central Government intends to take away your right to vote in the GLC elections? **SAY NO TO NO SAY.**

prompted the Tory government to set up the Widdicombe committee to report on the legitimacy of local authorities using ratepayers' money on publicity drives.

The story began in November, 1983, with a ten minute Conservative Party TV broadcast outlining the abolition programme for local authorities. With Local Government Minister Kenneth Baker comfortably defending the logic of the proposal, few members of the Cabinet could, at that time, have anticipated the venom with which their "rationalisation" proposals would be met. It was a battle that would spill over both sides of the political fence in the House of Commons, invade the House of Lords and inflame the passions of the media for almost two years. The GLC and six metropolitan councils were lined up for the chop.

Within a month, the GLC had decided to take unprecedented political action. They would go down fighting, hiring an advertising agency to put their message across. Tony Wilson, the GLC's head of publicity, recalls that the decision came out of a long, all-party, all-afternoon meeting. That in itself was an achievement, as Wilson points out: "Advertising goes against the grain of the radical". The fear that the exorbitant costs of advertising would alienate councillors from their constituents was also finally overruled by the recollection of

Thatcher's "devastation of Labour at the last election". It was time to play Thatcher at her own game.

On January 1, 1984, the GLC was in the unfortunate position of not having an advertising agency to back its resolution. NCK (Norman, Craig, Kummel) had been fired, following their purchase by Foote, Cone and Belding, a bigger agency with unacceptable interests in South Africa. In the scout round for an acceptable alternative, BMP (Boas, Massimi, Pollitt) came up. Account Director Peter Herd suggests that they were given the GLC account on the strength of their track record for the white collar union NALGO and other local government groups. He describes the meeting as a "low level competition pitch" because "there wasn't time to put forward proposals – at that time we had no idea of the budgets or what was involved."

Herd, obviously familiar with the question "Can you market politics like soap powder?" says there is basically no difference: "Developing advertising in a political context is just the same as developing it in a commercial context. You find out a progression of what it is you can reasonably achieve, who you will have to persuade in order to do that, and then research to find out what is most likely to affect them. That is the process we went through with the GLC, as we would with Cadburys,

Courage or the *Guardian*. It's the same process."

BMP's long history as a research-based agency means that the market research function is built into the agency mix. Herd's account planner came up with very similar findings to the MORI and Harris polls which had indicated that around forty per cent of Londoners were opposed to the abolition of the GLC. Of the rest, "well over fifty per cent either didn't know or didn't care about the GLC." With this kind of depressing information in hand, BMP set about creating a campaign strategy. Herd recalls: "It became clear from the research groups that most people weren't interested in the GLC or government proposals. But the one thing that they did get excited about on the abolition issue was the government's plan to take their vote away. That inspired people despite the fact that most of them had never used their vote, or didn't know they had it anyway. The great British democratic tradition flared up."

GLC press officer Nita Clarke says that the strategy evolved in two parts. In addition to the need to "raise awareness" about abolition, the GLC wanted to promote information about the job the Council did. As a result, adverts went out promoting organisations like the fire service, sponsored events like rock concerts and summer festivals, and "social issues"

like claimants' rights and pavement parking. Much of this work was done "in house", leaving BMP free to get on with the business of abolition.

The first part of the anti-abolition campaign was to focus on the "serious" theme of the erosion of democracy. "We wanted the tone to be not what people might expect from the GLC," says Herd. "The opposite of the looney lefty image. The early stuff was very earnest and responsible." This sincerity reflected itself in the visual style chosen for the campaign. Copy lines ran from "From Now On You Have No Say In Who Runs London" through to "What Kind Of Place Is It That Takes Away Your Right To Vote And Leaves You With No Say?" The images used lots of heavy, "important" upper case lettering, black lines and simple stark images. The black and white became a hallmark of the GLC campaign. Ironically, this decision was taken because BMP simply didn't have the time to get posters run in colour; but feedback from consumer research suggested unanimous approval. The punters felt that black and white conveyed a serious tone and reflected cost-cutting economy.

Because of its political content, the anti-abolition campaign was in fact restricted to press and posters. The IBA (which oversees commercial radio and TV) states quite categorically that "no advertisement may be inserted by or

Picture opposite:

"If You Want Me Out" represented a turning point in Boas Massimi Pollitt's anti-abolition campaign for the GLC. Even arch enemies of "Red Ken" could not dispute the logic and democratic commonsense of the advert.

"IF YOU WANT ME OUT YOU SHOULD HAVE THE RIGHT TO VOTE ME OUT."

Everyone's entitled to their view. The British constitution says you express it through the ballot box.

That's the law.

Unfortunately the Government doesn't like the law as it stands in relation to the GLC.

Today the first bill relating to the abolition of the GLC gets its second reading in the House.

It's devised to wipe out next year's GLC elections. Whether you're Labour, Tory, Liberal or SDP, you'll have no say.

Not since the last World War has your statutory right to vote been withdrawn in this way.

And it's a cynical dismissal of public opinion.

In a recent MORI poll 61% of Londoners of all political persuasions said no.

Only 22%, by the way, said yes.

In every straw poll, overwhelming public opinion has said no to abolition.

On 26th March Tom King the Conservative Secretary for Employment outlined in the House the elementary rights of people to register their vote without interference.

That was in relation to the Trade Union movement.

This Government steadfastly refuses to apply the same principles to the rights of 7 million Londoners.

You may hold the view of course,

that they were voted into power democratically and have the right to do as they wish.

But, nowhere in the Tory manifesto was there a mention of abolishing your right to vote in local elections.

Ask yourself why the Government is intent on doing away with the GLC in the first place.

There has not been a single proposition motivated by the desire to improve London.

What you might have heard have been outbursts.

"Red Ken spending our money on weirdos again."

(For the record less than half of one

per cent of GLC expenditure is allocated to all minorities.)

Don't let bigoted arguments of this kind blind you to the real issue.

This country's centuries old democratic tradition is at stake.

Local Government is one of the checks and balances which safeguard us against the abuse of central Government power.

And it would be an abuse of power for any Government to abolish a democratic institution such as a local authority, simply because it did not like the incumbent administration.

SAY NO TO NO SAY.

on behalf of anybody, the objects whereof are wholly or mainly of a political nature, and no advertisement may be directed towards any political end."

With a favourable wind blowing from the MORI polls and BMP's own research, the agency moved into a second phase. "It was time for some humour," says Herd, the double aim being to ridicule the Tories and make the GLC look humane. One of the most effective adverts of the early stage was the simple mug shot of Ken Livingstone stating: "If you want me out you should have the right to vote me out." People now started to look out for the next GLC ad; gradually they became a cult.

This second phase witnessed a shift from the theme of democracy to one of central-isation. By now it was the summer of 1984 and parliament was about to go into summer recess. Herd says that they wanted to capitalise on this. "We decided to pre-empt the government argument that abolition was democratic because it gave power back to the boroughs. It's patently not true; so we spent three months saying that abolition meant centralisation." The result was a spate of anti-Whitehall ads, conveying the message that talking to Whitehall is like talking to a brick wall, moving at a snail's pace, etc. The opinion polls reported an upsurge, allowing BMP to run its clincher ad: "Seventy-four per cent say No."

Inevitably the success of the GLC campaign put the wind up the government. In January, 1985, the courts put a temporary ban on GLC advertising; and the Tories commissioned the Widdicombe report. Herd regards this move as ironic. "It's quite extraordinary that the Conservative Party, which brought the skills of advertising to politics, should now be trying to stop it," he says, a bizarre situation further compounded by the parallel collapse of the left's traditional resistance to the use of the media: "And it was a far left group, not the moderates, who actually took up advertising."

As we will see later in this chapter, the "liberal" Widdicombe report on local authority spending on publicity was to be all but ignored by the government. Whereas David Widdicombe and his committee had recommended in the July 1985 interim report that "it is right for local authorities to be able to explain their views on controversial matters affecting them ... including issuing information about abolition and ratecapping", the ensuing Local Government Bill challenged its findings and argued for massive restrictions on both paid and unpaid local government publicity.

Although in the summer of 1985 the GLC had spent £2.5 million on the anti-abolition campaign, and a further £10 million (in 1984–1985) on advertising services and facilities, they maintained that the most important aspect of the campaign was the "free" advertising they'd received from press coverage in newspapers, public debates and news spots on Thames TV. The government, meanwhile, is determined that not only should publicity funded by the rate base be abolished, but also that "free" publicity expressing local government's "political" perspective should be curtailed.

The GLC's Nita Clarke outlined the importance of "free" publicity, which carries more credibility than paid-for advertising: "The advertising wouldn't have worked without the press support, whilst conversely the advertising made anti-abolition 'an issue' which the press needed to take seriously."

Shifting press opinion about the GLC was in fact to prove more difficult than shifting the public. The solution was to "target market stories", or "horses for courses" as Nita Clarke puts it. They fed items on democracy to the *Guardian*, debates about efficiency to the *Daily Telegraph* and "stunts" to the taboids. The whole operation was tactical, geared to prompting the press not only to sway public opinion, but more strategically the view of "opinion makers". As a consequence they would schedule stories, posters and press ads

to run a few days before the abolition Bill's discussion in Parliament.

Over eighteen months, most of the press did a remarkable U-turn, eventually condemning abolition on the grounds of democracy, efficiency, etc. The biggest coup was the *Standard*. The GLC's Tony Wilson recalls: "They were our biggest enemy, but in the early days they did a poll of their own and discovered that most Londoners were against abolition. So in the interests of their readers – or rather to protect their readership figures – they couldn't come out against abolition." Wilson argues that the advertising can be indirectly credited for this: "Advertising does have a direct effect on editorial environment. The more we spent on advertising the more editorial copy ran, and the more it supported us." He doesn't see this as an act of manipulation, pointing out that advertising "didn't change the press' attitude, what it did was to make them realise that abolition was an important 'newsworthy issue' and that there was a debate to be had."

Meanwhile, Ken Livingstone was himself becoming a newsworthy item. The leader of the GLC had achieved a historical first, making the leader of a council a public and, eventually, much loved figure. His immense PR capabilities are endorsed by BMP's Peter Herd, who laughs at the proposition that they "modelled his public image" along the lines of Thatcher's Gordon Reece. "Livingstone is the cleverest manipulator of public relations in the history of politics. Quite without our assistance he turned from being the ogre of the left into a charming chat show host."

The success of the GLC campaign has not passed the notice of the trade unions, some of whom are at long last waking up to the importance of "cost effective communication". Unions like NALGO, USDAW (retail and distribution) and the American AFSCME have already set the pace, and other local authorities, like Derbyshire (also run by BMP), have taken up the gauntlet. The TUC decided in early 1986, for example, to spend £250,000 on a campaign (agency: Delaney, Fletcher, Delaney) against threatened sackings at Cheltenham's GCHQ.

The cost of employing a commercial agency can obviously be prohibitive – £2 million is well beyond the reach of most unions. But even on a limited budget, Tony Wilson argues that lessons have been learned. He cites the example of the TUC's recent campaign to retain the political levy: "The TUC was under pressure from the union leaders to come up with a GLC Mark Two. What in fact they did was the opposite, but the same background research principles applied. We decided we needed to raise the public profile of the GLC. TUC research, on the other hand,

indicated that they needed to lower their profile. They couldn't use the press, who have a confirmed anti-union political levy stance, so their focus was the workplace." Research also indicated that many unions were, and still are, anti-Labour. So the TUC campaign raised the need for a political levy but didn't mention Labour or socialist policies. Wilson maintains that such research is essential: "Find out your strengths and weaknesses, what sells and what doesn't."

The priority given to market research by the GLC highlights a marked departure from traditional left thinking about the role of advertising, and an acceptance of the concepts of strategy, planning, and incorporating the beliefs and assumptions of the potential consumer into the "marketing mix". Peter Herd goes a stage further, arguing that "feedback from the consumer is an essential part of the democratic process. It's naive to suggest that these services which advertising provides work only to benefit private profit and capitalism ... Following on from the GLC campaign, I can envisage a time when the left does a U-turn. After years of condemning advertising, they'll decide it's a good thing. But it's not anything in itself. It can be a good or a bad thing. Intention matters, it's what you say, how you say it, and the point which cannot be ignored, how much money you have to spend."

Postscript

The preceding interview took place in August, 1985, shortly after the release of the Widdicombe Report on local authority spending. By November the situation had changed dramatically. The Environment Minister Kenneth Baker launched the Local Government Bill with the words: "Rates were never meant to fund the personal ego trips of a handful of councillors who use their spending power at local level to create a springboard to further their own political careers at a national level." The most controversial part of the Bill comes in Part Two, referring to local authority publicity. It states: "A local authority shall not publish any material which in whole or in part, appears to be designed to affect, or can reasonably be regarded as likely to affect, public support for a) a political party or b) a body, cause or campaign identified with, or likely to be regarded as identified with a political party."

Rhetoric which, if interpreted to the letter, would prohibit local authorities from publishing, or funding any organisation that publishes material which may appear to affect public support, not only for a political party, but also for any organisation "identified" as political. That could at one swipe not only rule out support for anti-racial, sexual, political, ecology, legal rights groups, but could also jeopardise "general" information and publicity about events and facilities available – if their publicisation could be proved to be inspired by a "political" motivation. Part b) of the above was later deleted, but the implications of the Bill still remain intact.

As the PPA (Periodical Publishers' Association) pointed out in their draft Code of Practice for advertising agencies, publicity under the Bill is defined as "any communication, in whatever form, addressed to the public at large or a section of the public." This would therefore include paid publicity, including paid advertising in the press, on radio and television, leaflets, campaign exhibitions, as well as unpaid publicity, including council and committee reports, consultation documents, press releases, press conference statements, media interviews, etc. In other words, the Bill could be used effectively to silence the government's critics and stifle public debate over a controversial issue.

This throws into sharp relief the overlap between advertising, propaganda and information. Clearly the Bill aims to interpret all "controversial" information and advertising issued by local councils as propaganda, mooting this as justifiable grounds for censorship. Precisely at the point where the left has considered using the media as an acceptable and useful

SACRIFICE ?

THE MAN AT THE TOP:-
"Equality of Sac-
rifice—that's the
big idea, friends!
Let's all
step down
one rung!"

THE
UNEMPLOYED
MAN

From "PLEBS" (the Organ of the N.C.L.C.)

VOTE LABOUR

social voice, the right is intent on clamping down on the means of communication.

2: The Labour Party

John Gorman's book, *Images of Labour*, is packed with an archive of trade union banners, badges, posters, postcards, commemoration mugs and assorted political ephemera – a testimony to the movement's creativity and propaganda. Much of this material is quite arresting – specifically, and not surprisingly, the art work of the 1930s, where there appears to have been an intense co-incidence of "modern" creative talent and political commit-ment. Retrospectively, this can be seen as a pioneering period for propaganda, giving birth to the arguments for "new", socially progressive visual languages with which to trail-blaze the revolution. As we've already seen, photo-montage was a child of that debate.

Sadly, nothing more recently in the book matches that creative inspiration. Ephemera to commemorate later periods is thin, or missing. This is partly due to the author's natural focus but, more im-portantly, to the fact that Labour has increasingly in-habited a creative wasteland. Gorman's postscript sums up the dilemma. Describing a union national conference at which a proposed publicity record by Acker Bilk was discussed, he quotes a shop steward from Nottingham as saying: "I don't see why we should waste our money on pop records".

Since the early 1970s, Labour's suspicion of adver-tising has been further coloured by an increasingly "right" media tone. Treatment of trade unions in particular has been extensively exposed by the Glasgow Media Group, among others. But alongside this suspicion, the radical left witnessed a new creative flourishing. The massive arts grants base of the 1970s made possible the evolution of a nationwide network of "alter-native" art centres: Camera-work, Bootle, Watershed, The Side Gallery, etc. The same funding base also created posts for community artists, community photographers and an "alternative" visual prac-tice.

But it also has to be pointed out that this "alternative" sector, as its ambitions be-came more sweeping, radical and impassioned, dislocated itself from the main Labour movement. With the exception of photographers and artists directly committed to the movement (producing "ac-ceptable" worker documentary photographs of circa 1930 montages) the alternative sector threatened the sensi-bilities of Labour as much as the sophisticated chic of the modern media. Labour was fragmented and isolated, an observation borne out by the

Tory landslide of 1979. Labour no longer seemed to represent the worker. It certainly didn't represent the political interests of the intellectual avant-garde, nor for that matter a number of subsets ushered under its umbrella: women, blacks, the old, etc. Labour was a mess. It didn't know its constituency, nor the language with which to address them. This internal confusion had the inevitable effect of cutting Labour off from its creative life-blood.

As Stuart Hall has commented: "The elements are around us in the fragments waiting to be used. People have a lot of skills and want to use them. Those skills need to be harnessed. It's less important where they come from, as how they can be used. I mean you just have to walk into the Labour Party headquarters, and you instantly know what's wrong, they're just not tuned in. People with the necessary skills are available for socialism. You see it in film, in journalism, in community arts, all over the place. But they're divorced from the traditional labour movement." (*Camerawork*, 29)

* * * * * *

The decision both to co-ordinate the party and give Labour a "corporate image" goes back to some months before the last general election in June, 1983. The preceding January, Labour had cemented its hotly disputed commitment to media management through the appointment of a new head of advertising, Nick Grant, and the employment of a commercial advertising agency – Wrights – who had handled the 1982 campaign on unemployment. This depicted a rising unemployment graph captioned "See what happens when you don't vote Labour". It was one stab against the Tories' carefully choreographed image making. Nick Grant reflects: "1981–2 had been bad years for Labour in terms of the internal disputes, and in the opinion polls, which the Tories had favourably harvested from the Falklands war. We decided to run a pre-election campaign designed to pull people's ideas back together again about Labour."

As a result of what Grant calls the "internal party decision making processes", this was delayed and mismanaged. In the event the campaign didn't break until the end of April, a delay of almost two months. Local authority elections threatened at the end of May, so the Wright campaign now had to fight a local government issue as well. Internal and MORI research suggested three important issues:
1. People felt hopeless about the future.
2. People felt helpless to change it.
3. With four out of five people still working there was no point in solely addressing the unemployed. Equally, people in employment

Pictures opposite:
The 1930s saw popular crusades against unemployment.

THINK POSITIVE VOTE LABOUR.

THINK POSITIVE. ACT POSITIVE VOTE LABOUR.

didn't want to think about the plight of the unemployed.

Wrights came up with a three point strategy.

1. Bringing home to people that being in work was a fragile situation likely to change.
2. That with Labour it was possible to change things.
3. That polling day mattered.

The creative strategy resulted in such copy lines as "Are you going to vote yourself out of a job?" "Are you going to vote your children out of a future?" and "Are you going to vote for the death of the NHS?" The effectiveness of this campaign is still disputed. Many felt that the stark, depressing montages alienated the public. Opinion poll research suggested that many of the adverts, especially the children on a trash heap (a theme later picked up by the *Mirror* newspaper) went down well. Whilst much blame has been laid at the feet of Wrights for not coming up with a good enough campaign, Grant is the first to maintain that it was Labour Party inefficiency which created the problems. Everything had to be monitored and approved by the campaign committee, and "trying to get forty people to agree on anything is very difficult."

But whatever the strengths of Wright's pre-election campaign, it was not equipped to deal with the Tories' decision to run the general election so soon after the May local government poll. Grant says:

"We had a choice to make. Whether to change gear completely with a new campaign or whether it would be better to continue with the pre-election campaign, having spent so much money on it."

The results of the election are known – a massive Conservative landslide. Shortly after the Thatcher victory, *Panorama* scheduled a remarkable documentary, "The Marketing of Margaret", which looked at how her media image had been fed, fostered and cultivated before the elections. Like Reagan, she had employed professionals. Saatchi and Saatchi on advertising, ex-Mars bar baron Christopher Lawson as Director of Marketing, Gordon Reece (fresh from observing Reagan) on voice and appearance. The team was unmatchable, and *Panorama* could justifiably introduce the programme with: "The way that the party image is presented, sold if you like, matters equally as much as policies or personalities."

Labour's response was mixed. It could not wholly condemn advertising because it had employed Wrights. The case was argued on the grounds of manipulation. Labour had fought and lost on issues. Thatcher had lied and employed the media to package the wolf in sheep's clothing, a faulty product in a fresh pack. Labour's Jim Mortimer was able to say with conviction: "I can assure you that the Labour Party will never follow such a line of presentation in politics for very serious reasons: the welfare of human beings, the care of people and the fact that we want to overcome unemployment. These are the real tasks before us, not presenting people as if they were breakfast food or baked beans."

With Labour's back against the wall, two issues had become confused. The human "care" issue had overshadowed the fact that whatever the message, Thatcher's campaign had been brilliantly marketed, organised and thought out. Consumer feedback was thrown into the marketing mix at every stage of the operation. These were skills which could equally well have been harnessed for Labour had they had the resources, organisation and, in the end, respect for their audience: an audience reared on computers, not abacuses.

The issue inevitably raised the old war horse of selling politics like detergent. The Conservatives' Christopher Lawson was unequivocal: "The big difference in marketing party political policies [from a commodity] is that one has much less to say about what goes into the product; but otherwise it's the same." Nick Grant agrees, with qualification, distinguishing between the marketing – the essence of advertising – and the images and values which a consumer culture purveys. "The easy poke, that we're not going to sell Labour like we sell soap powder, quite frankly doesn't gell. It's so old fashioned to assume that advertising, the media and opinion research has nothing to do with communicating with voters. If you don't adopt those sort of tactics you're depriving yourself of finding out what people are thinking." This "consumer information," Grant argues, is essential to the democratic process. "The only alternative is mass door-stepping – which you have to collate – or a politician's nose and the hunches of the people he's surrounded by." It's an argument with which both the GLC and the agency BMP would be in sympathy.

But despite the "democratic" appeal of market research, it still meets with fundamental objections within Labour thinking. Grant's assertion that "they don't like opinion polls because they don't like the findings" only goes part of the way to providing an answer. Many Labour Party members fundamentally distrust the "scientific" quantification of social values, preferring the "hands on" approach of personal contact and door-stepping. The Party's pre-election "in house" video, *The Socialist Alternative*, put the position well: "The campaign starts here today... we depend on party members to get the message across, at work or in the pub or on the door-step." This humanitarian, local community level of self help is, after all, fundamental to Labour

Pictures opposite:

Are you voting yourself out of the election? These images didn't win the last election, nor were they supposed to. Originally drummed up by Wrights agency for a spring publicity drive, they had by the summer served for the by-elections and the general election of June, 1983. Trading on a nostalgia for the workers' movement and the formality of 1930s montage, many people said the ads were dated, portraying a depressing, defensive image of the Labour Party. The Labour Party campaign machine thought otherwise, approving them as part of the party's tentative move towards "commercial" campaigning.

thinking, and in many people's eyes what differentiates socialism from the "faceless" profit motive of Thatcherism.

But market research is also more than "simply bouncing ideas off the consumer" or finding out "what the consumer wants". Effective market research starts with a vision of what is required and demands the interpretation and manipulation of the findings. There is no such thing as "pure" science. After all, if Labour had given the voter "what they wanted" at the last election, they would have given them a Tory government. The GLC's Tony Wilson made no bones about the fact that manipulation, in a good cause, was a valid strategy. Nick Grant thinks similarly: "Of course advertising is manipulative. The whole point is to make it manipulative on our behalf. People, in my opinion, make a fallacious distinction between propaganda which is alright and advertising which isn't. One of the questions you have to ask yourself about why people in business make money, is because they are a shrewd judge of the way that profits work. They play the system better, they know that advertising works and that's why they invest in it."

Grant will not, however, be drawn into the trap of "anything goes". He doesn't believe that in order to sell politics it is necessary to reproduce hackneyed, outworn social stereo-types, or promote false values. "The idea of using stereotypes and luxury images is only the conventional view of advertising. It is advertising used to sell a product. We are selling a set of social values. What you have to do is substitute the offending aspiration for one you've researched. One that is harmonious with your socialist principles. So, for example, we've seen through research that people aren't seeking huge personal wealth, they're after job security; an economy that works for them. Selling a philosophy, because it is intangible, is much more complex than selling a product. All we are endorsing about advertising is the narrow, highly methodological technique. We are not endorsing the style, the form or any particular way of advertising a product. We're trying to extract and benefit from the scientific techniques of marketing and apply it to a different world."

Many people inside and outside the Labour Party have criticised the fact that under Nick Grant's two-year tenure of office little was effected. The election campaign is almost unanimously seen as a disaster, and Wrights and Grant incriminated. But whatever the personal failings, it is patently obvious that you cannot simply graft modern marketing techniques on to an old, "democratic", forty-strong committee who believe in traditional methods of communication. This problem is exacerbated by the lack of revenue.

Labour has since appointed Peter Mandalson from London Weekend Television to become its new head of Communications and Campaigns, part of an internal reshuffle by General Secretary Larry Whitty. Mandalson says he believes in traditional methods of advertisig, publicity events, training politicians to be "media happy" and endeavouring to burnish up the image of "Neil Appeal". He sees his job as internal reorganisation, a redistribution of labour, the design of an effective communications strategy, and finally its implementation. The design is promised for the spring of 1986, and the implementation will be effected over the following couple of years. For that, we shall have to wait.

3: City Limits

City Limits was not a magazine "born" in the traditional sense. It did not spring from in-depth analysis of the market, researched financial planning or a coherent editorial vision. It emerged from a staff dispute over working conditions and wage parity within London's *Time Out* listings and entertainment magazine during the spring and summer of 1981. As this dispute polarised, the striking staff produced an alternative fly sheet entitled *Not Time Out*. By the following October, they had managed to start a new magazine – *City Limits*.

Within an amazingly short time, funding was raised from a variety of sources. The GLC advanced a loan of £80,000 to the newly formed collective. Contrary to popular opinion this was also issued at a commercial rate of interest, and not as a grant or gift. In addition, the staff raised £50,000 in loans from well-wishers, again at a commercial rate of interest. £50,000 more came from outside shareholders, and the immediate cash flow from the magazine's cover price and advertising revenue. However, many commercial magazines launch on "start up" funding of between £500,000 and £1,000,000; with few resources to fall back on, *City Limits* needed to break even as soon as possible.

The first year was the most difficult, with staff taking pay cuts to weather the commercial storm. In addition to normal teething problems, the magazine was further blighted by boycotts from advertisers who either took a political objection to the socialist principles of the magazine, favoured *Time Out* for historical reasons, or argued that *City Limits* failed to provide an adequate circulation/readership to make advertising financially viable. This was a Catch 22, because until the magazine had been in business for a year or so, providing adequate market information about the readership would be

Pictures opposite:

Labour's Jobs and Industry Campaign. Stunned by the 1983 election defeat, the party started to regenerate support at a grass roots level. The Jobs and Industry Campaign spawned a host of stickers, labels, pamphlets and information packs targeted at specific groups of workers: for example, the motor industry, or workers in the West Midlands. The design of this material was simple, functional and educational, produced in the de rigeur socialist colours of black and red.

CITY LIMITS MARCH 20-27   233   70p

CITY LIMITS MAGAZINE

FREEZE FRAME
WHY IS THE COLD WAR BACK IN THE MOVIES?

PATRICIA HIGHSMITH on guilt-edged males
'THE WHISTLE BLOWER' on location at GCHQ
WIN! A Transylvanian VAMPIRE holiday
FREE! Tickets to 'FRIGHTNIGHT'

impossible.

In addition to these external problems, it has taken the magazine several years to thrash out an advertising policy. This partly involves what kind of adverts should be taken, partly the internal organisation of the advertising department. Indeed, it is only now, with the magazine in its fourth year, and well past its 200th edition, that many of these issues are being thrashed out – a move accelerated by the imminent collapse of the GLC, traditionally an important source of advertising revenue.

The kind of advertising a "socialist" magazine should take is complicated for several reasons. As already mentioned, City Limits was initially fighting a rearguard action against advertisers who sided with Time Out over the dispute, and felt that the rebellious image of City Limits was "wrong" for their product. In addition, with a circulation peaking at 25,000 but sometimes as low as 18,000 (although readership can be estimated as double or quadruple this), the magazine could not supply the readership which many large brand name advertisers were demanding. Finally, the magazine itself had a policy of not accepting adverts whose language or product was thought to be offensive to the social groups whose interests City Limits sought to represent.

Both John McDermott and Roy Patterson, advertising and marketing managers respect-ively during 1985, agree on the last point: that the language of advertising is less of a problem than the kind of product advertised. This is for the simple reason that adver-tisers are in the business of selling goods, and a "sexist or racist advert would be com-mercial suicide for a magazine like City Limits." Patterson argues that because advertisers have no "political axe to grind" they are frequently ready and willing to change the copy or image on an advert. "They see it simply in terms of target marketing. The wrong image will not shift their product." Patterson cites cases of film companies who've delivered ads whose "victim" images of women in horror films could be offensive. "Not only that, but the wrong image could put a lot of our readers off from seeing an otherwise good film. Advertisers recognise that it's in their interests to change the ad." McDermott feels there is rarely a case for turning an offensive ad away. Usually a chat on the phone will produce a fresh response: "Censorship rarely achieves anything".

The problem of products is slightly different. There have at various times been discus-sions within the magazine on the need to boycott all South African invested companies. Cigarette advertising has also proved contentious, as has whether or not the classified section should break the law and take ads from under-age gay men. Patterson feels that

Picture opposite:
Cover of City Limits

it's a matter of judgement: "You can only face the visible enemy, like Rothman's or Barclays Bank. Once you get on to multinationals the issue becomes much more complicated. You find hundreds of firms have investments in politically questionable countries." Ultimately, in order to survive, the magazine needs to sell ad space. With a current rate card of £665 per page, Patterson argues that "*City Limits* has to prove itself out there in the jungle. It has to go out on the news stands and dig the dirt with the rest of the girls."

Public acceptability of *City Limits* has been a slow process. For several years advertisers fought shy of the magazine, seduced by the image of lefties as broke, *Guardian*-reading students who spent their money on causes rather than commodities. This image of *City Limits* as a campaigning magazine for the disaffected also inspired part of the magazine's workers' self image. So it has been as much a problem for the staff as for the advertisers to come to terms with market research data which suggests that the readers are, in fact, primarily in the ABC1 range, and tend to have high disposable incomes. As Patterson points out: "The left tend to be the perfect consumer, obsessed with commodities and entertainment because they have rejected traditional middle class spending patterns." In effect, this means that they don't deposit their money in "invisible" investments like insurance, private education, pension plans, etc.

This image of the left as consumers is perhaps the hardest fact to accept. "*City Limits* is much more interested in production than it is in consumption," says Patterson. "Which is a real Marxist problem. All of the effort is put into producing the product, making sure that it hits the streets each week, as opposed to stepping back and asking how it is consumed by the public. What the consumer wants is very much a secondary consideration. This is the opposite of commercial thinking, where the first question would be 'Where's the market?'... *City Limits* is not about politics primarily, it is about lifestyle. That is what a listings magazine is. How to spend your money and your time." Patterson also feels that whilst the actual market for a listings magazine can at best enlarge slowly, the advertising revenue potential for *City Limits* can steadily improve. Nor does he see its left-wing image as a problem. "If you've got a viable product that is selling socialism and 150,000 copies a week, advertisers couldn't give a fuck about the politics. In that sense you can use capitalism against itself."

Not surprisingly, some of Patterson's "commercial" ideas are out of step with the philosophy of other workers on the magazine. This broad spectrum of left opinion is the magazine's weakness, and also its strength. Rather than representing one unified line, it is eclectic and catholic in the range of political opinions it will tolerate. It is this lack of dogma, rarely identified as a feature of left politics, which gives the magazine its vitality and strength. It also guarantees it a foothold in a host of not always compatible groups: feminists, gays, liberals, blacks, educationalists, and individuals who treat the magazine more as a sounding board than a rule book. Ironically perhaps, the collapse of the GLC, and the loss of a small but regular source of advertising revenue, has now forced the magazine to rethink its advertising policy in the light of market research information about who the consumers are, and what they want.

Picture left:
The famous Futon, and other well-upholstered pine sprung small ads provided the backbone of *City Limits* income in the early days. Whilst the big advertisers blacklisted or ignored the *City Limits'* readership as irrelevant, small entrepreneurial companies recognised the importance of a broad-based left readership for sales. After all, even socialists buy beds, eat out, watch movies and consume culture.

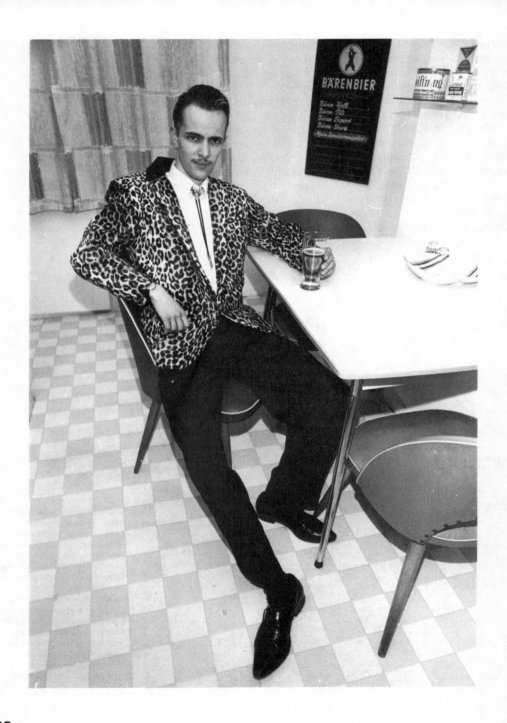

6

TOWARDS A THEORY OF CONSUMPTION

1: Excess: the tale of the apple

MANY OF THE criticisms fired at advertising are in fact criticisms of consumerism: the "spend, spend, spend" philosophy of capitalism. As the *City Limits* example showed, it's necessary to draw a line between *consumption* and rampant *consumerism*. After all, even under socialism people will want to consume. Pleasure and comfort play an integral part in culture. But before it's possible to distinguish between consumption and consumerism, it's necessary to back track over the debates which pushed the persuasive Eve, and her supermarket trolley full of apples, out of the socialist garden.

Most of the left's persistent criticism of "excess" is valid. With three-quarters of the world near starvation, it is hard to justify the endless purchase of cosmetics, new cars, food processors, microwave cookers and luxury foods. As Reyner Banham acidly remarked in his obituary to "household gadgets": "Have you ever checked how short a time the average domestic washer operates in the average week? There would be a nationwide scandal if any mechanical plant in the public domain were so under-employed. And have you actually read the instructions on the new liquidiser: Maximum operating time 45 seconds, followed by a shutdown of at least a minute. Even in the first rapture of ownership, a plant like this may not run as much as ten minutes in a month." (*Art in Society*, ed. Paul Barker, 1977)

It is not so easy, however, to decide what is a socially necessary commodity. At its simplest there are clothes, heat, food and shelter; but in an advanced technological society most of these needs should at least be met. The

Picture opposite:

The shock of the new is too much for the left. The fear of becoming a modern consumer, a capitalist cog, is coupled with a passionate reverence for the production line promise of the past. 1950s and 1960s chic is the new junk avant garde. In 1986 Brylcreem, Dansettes, stilettos, Bush trannies, plastic dinner-ware, plastic hoop earrings and kitsch cocktail shakers are the right stuff. Picture by Mike Hughes.

problem becomes more complicated when discriminating between different cuts of coat, different styles of housing or different kinds of food. At what point does a decision based on a principle of style, taste or fashion move from the necessary to the excessive? Is the "aesthetic" arguably as important a consideration as the "function"?

As we've seen already, consumption – why and how people consume goods – has never been treated as an important part of economic theory. This is because consumption is thought to be a "reactive" process, quite crudely reacting to the fruits of industry – that which has already been produced. The only exception to this is price, where "excess demand" can force the price of a good up, or in the reverse, down. Most economists would agree that consumers rarely have any influence over what kind of good is produced by manufacturers. And this theory that consumption is "outside" economics also affects the way in which the left sees and understands the role of commodities in our lives. It links up inextricably with the idea that the world is divided into socially useful and useless goods, and that advertising is responsible for the stage management of the latter.

It's worth at this point digressing into some aspects of economic theory, specifically Marx's distinction between "use value" and "exchange value", as a basis for understanding the difference between useful and useless (or rather, fashion-determined) commodities. For Marx, every commodity produced under capitalist modes of organisation possesses a dual aspect: a "use value" and an "exchange value". Use value is essentially functional, for example the use value of a coat is its ability to keep its wearer warm. Use value, then, expresses a relation between objects and people. By comparison, exchange value refers to the value which a product has when it is offered in exchange for other goods. On one level, this might be perceived as simply a relation between objects, but Marx emphasised that this level of appearances is simply the commodities' "fetish form". For Marx, relations between objects work to conceal the fundamental relationships between men who invested their labour to produce those commodities. Exchange value is, therefore, a measure of the labour invested in a commodity, fundamentally a social relationship between people, as opposed to use value, which is expressed as a relation between people and objects. Marx recognised that a certain amount of "useful" labour must be expended in order to create use values for commodities but, fundamentally, use value is only realised in the act of consumption. To put it simply, exchange value expresses the relation between commodities and productive labour, and use value expresses the relation between commodities and consumers.

As I've already suggested, within orthodox Marxist theory consumption is subordinated to production as a determining force. As a consequence, within the political economy of Marxism, use value is decentred from the analysis of capitalist rationale because it expresses "consumer object relations" as opposed to productive social relations. Clearly, an understanding of use value has to shift away from an interpretation of needs and wants as purely physiological or biological in origin (for example food and warmth), and from a notion of use value as an inherent characteristic of an object or commodity. Commodities and needs are social in origin. To explain consumer choice (for example between a series of coats which perform an identical "warmth keeping" function) in a highly sophisticated market economy, we have to be able to assess not only what a product does, but also what it means. The construction of use values, and the transformation of these values into meanings identifiable by the consumer, therefore constitutes the central role of advertising agency practice. The act of producing values and meanings simultaneously provides identities for commodities and consumers.

The basic point is quite simple. Advertising has realised something which has eluded orthodox economic theory at both ends of the political spectrum. Use values are not outside the economy at all. You only have to look at the launch for a new product to realise this point. Use value – defining basic needs – is as much part of the marketing mix as designing the packaging: Ovaltine and Horlicks, for example, whose use to the consumer as a sleepy time drink, as a health restorative and as a nerve calmer, has fluctuated with the economy and the strength of brand competitors. Or Energen crispbread, where marketing and advertising defined the basic "use" for the product, moving it from a "diet" food to part of a "sensible" diet, bypassing on the way the option of becoming a "natural" or "health" food. In terms of advertising structure, the need to define "use" is an essential part of every campaign and will appear on every creative brief. "Use" is what gives the product its exclusivity in relation to other competitors: it defines the product's position on the market.

The idea that certain "basic" goods lie outside the advertising net and, by extension, the political economy, is an illusion. Even items like coal, carrots and potatoes are branded through supermarket and other retail outlets. Creating uses, however, is not simply a

RG 31 Radiogram
£31.10.0 inc. P.T.
Legs optional; 2 gns extra.

POPULAR 4-speed player; all records.
£11.10.0 inc. P.T.

RT 222
Portable transistor radio £15.10.0 inc. P.T.

identities and become necessary to us, is an emotive one. The left's optimism that there are certain goods which can be sold on the strength of "basic need" as opposed to "spurious want" in an advanced capitalist economy, is clearly misplaced. It also means that in a prospective socialist economy, natural needs would not automatically spring up. What is necessary is a social, economic or political decision, not a biological one.

2: Out of the consumer jungle: second-hand chic

The intellectual left's suspicion of advertising as responsible for the promotion of unnecessary tastes has an economic foundation. As Marx's theory of value points out, the exchange value of a commodity is not a pure assessment of its merits and worth as compared to other goods available on the market. Marx calls this level of appearances whereby value appears to be a property of a thing, "commodity fetishism". Hovis comes from a village bakery not a baking factory; Benson and Hedges comes from pure gold, not a tobacco field. This fetishism conceals the true value of the good, which is determined by the

functional process. As Judith Williamson's *Decoding Advertisements* argues, the process by which commodities take on rate of exploitation: how cheaply an entrepreneur can get an item made, and how much surplus value or profit he can extract from this process. So imports from Taiwan under a cheap price tag also carry the concealed message that non-unionised labour has sweated blood to produce them. This real and painful knowledge inspires much of the left's criticism of advertising as somehow responsible for creating the demand that enabled this kind of economic exploitation to go on.

This explains why the left actively supports co-operative and small scale private enterprise, where only "socially necessary" labour goes into the production of a good which has a recognised "use value": brown rice, health shoes, herbs, etc. All of these alternative industries thrive in political terms because they are not seen to be extracting surplus value from the worker through exploitation and, just as importantly, satisfying "real needs".

It also explains why the left has been so aptly described as a "second-hand" economy: the polytechnic lecturer's house full of upgraded junk (not antiques), second-hand clothes, recycled loo paper and pets from Battersea Dogs' Home. The key is "recycled".

In other words, the first owner is the person guilty of endorsing the labourer's exploitaton through the purchase of a "new" dishwasher, Hoover, car or dress. Second time around, the rate of exploitation has been erased. All that is left, the fruit of built-in obsolescence, is junk. On the principle of salvation, the alternative culture can reclaim the junk, the outcasts of society. Recycling carries the added side benefit of reincarnation. Eating off a fifty-year-old table or writing with a bakelite pen is a testimony to the value of the labour invested by the labourer. The left has thus become a museum for second-hand production line items: re-valuing the exploitation of the past without the guilt of having actually maintained the system through HP or first-time purchase.

The thrill of salvation also conceals a fundamental obsession with well-made goods. The purchase may be found on a junk stall, but this apparent worthlessness is once again a fetish form. A dog-tooth suit that "only cost ten quid" in Oxfam might in today's terms cost £200 to replace. Buying quality tailored gear on the cheap is partly a matter of thrift, but also testifies to the trendy left's inability to reconcile its pocket with its tastes, its tastes with its politics. Second-hand suits – masquerading as working class hero circa 1930 or landowner circa 1950 – not only provides

a convenient way out of the modern fashion jungle (C&A Man, etc.), but also provides a kind of class mobility, a sort of flirting with the politics of style usually denied or made taboo. It allows them to taste the frisson of class and privilege without being called a traitor.

The importance of junk culture to the left cannot be underestimated. It is the only way that it can consume openly and without shame. In a sort of aesthetic necrophilia, it has to ransack the past because it has no way of conceiving of the present, or the future.

This also means that the middle class intelligentsia, the trendy market-scouring left, grows increasingly alienated from the Labour voting core. For whilst the intelligentsia wallows in the mirage of Depression, wholesomeness and sense of community, the modern working class, spurred on by the memory of Macmillan and "You never had it so good", continue to crave new housing, gadgets and cars. Meanwhile, left intellectual thought continues to regard consumption as a lethal disease second only to AIDS.

As we've seen in previous chapters, the left *has* gone some way to developing a theory of consumption. But most often people's tastes and preferences – their lifestyle – have been seen as part of ideology – a state of false consciousness. In other words, the worker's obsession with

Above picture:

As part of the new Brylcreem campaign, GREY Limited's Jan Heron (copywriter) and Su Sareen (Art Director) came up with the idea of making three commercials using old 1960s Brylcreem advertising footage and re-mixing and re-editing them, using the latest video techniques and modern music.

consumption and how to spend the weekly wage packet is itself the product of ideology. Strip away the scales from their eyes and the workers would see their "true" relationship to society: namely production. The implications of this are clear. From a political standpoint, taking consumption seriously is a threat to the heart of production-based economics. It represents, in much left thinking, a kind of betrayal.

When consumption *has* been tackled, it's been addressed as the "thing" which maintains the status quo. Workers are sold unnecessary "luxury" items which appear to justify their exploitation and endorse their affluent worker status. In the writings of the Frankfurt School, and more recently in writing on popular culture, film and the media, we've witnessed a shift in the argument from the consumption of commodities to the impact of the consumption of culture. Indeed, much of the scorn poured on "soap" TV, American movies, home videos, etc., is based on the assumption that this kind of "couch potato" culture numbs the brain, silences dissent and lulls the worker into a suitably affable state of mind to confront "work" and "alienation" on a Monday morning. Paradoxically, this is also the opinion of the British bourgeoisie: the workers are mindless, they have no culture, you can't take them to the opera.

3: Feminism: suffering from consumption

This unhappy alliance between the left and the most conservative elements of British society over the "poverty" of mass taste (chips, beefburgers, flock wallpaper, pine face formica, crimplene and soap TV) had by the late 1960s almost halted political theory. The possibility of social change, of actually getting the masses to want anything better, seemed miles away. Ironically, the challenge was to come from within the broad spectrum of the left – from feminism. In their dissatisfaction with the status quo, women were forced to think through a theory of ideology, and inadvertently, a theory of consumption.

As Rosetta Brookes explains, consumption defines women's subordination. "The tendency which stereotypes the woman as domestic consumer and displaces her activity from visibility (as production) also makes her visible as the consumed, so that not only her actions but her very being are subordinated to men's ... If the worker sells himself in the sense that he is selling his life by selling his time, the model is selling her time because she is selling herself." ("Women Visible and Women Invisible", *Studio International*, 3/1977)

The recognition that consumption underpinned women's domestic servitude, and by

'ADVERTISING—STOP SELLING SEXISM'

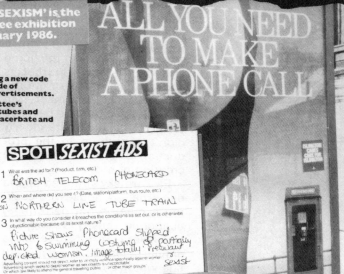

'ADVERTISING— STOP SELLING SEXISM' is the title of a GLC Women's Committee exhibition available for free loan from January 1986.

The exhibition features:

- **The Committee's achievement in securing a new code against sexism in London Transport's Code of Conditions Governing Acceptance of Advertisements.**

- **The complaints raised during the Committee's consultations with women about ads on tubes and buses, the feeling of insecurity the ads exacerbate and media sexism generally.**

- **The results of a SPOT SEXIST ADS monitoring exercise the Committee undertook to inform women of London Transport's changes to its code and to encourage passengers to note, if, how, when and where ads on tubes and buses continued, in their view, to be sexist.**

- **What makes an ad sexist and a grouping into five categories of those ads which attracted complaints.**

- **Examples of 'better practice' ads.**

- **Proposals for the contents of a code against sexism and the Women's Media Action Group's campaign for a code.**

Picture above:

The acceptable face of feminism. From the 1960s onwards, feminists have been in the vanguard of the critical assault on the methods, morality and meaning of advertising. Sexism has become a generic expression with which to criticise images which give women the status of objects on the one hand and on the other which define women exclusively as consumers, not producers of culture and commodities.

extension the nuclear family and "working" husband, resulted in a number of different strategies. The first, brought to light in tracts such as Anne Oakley's *Housewife* and Simone de Beauvoir's *The Second Sex* was that consumption is not regarded as "productive work". By extension, the "job" which women do all day in the home and in the supermarket is discredited, invisible from the economic balance sheet – an exclusion exonerated because women's labour quite clearly didn't contribute to the production of surplus value, the creation of profit.

Eli Zaretsky summed up the dilemma: "A housewife cooking a meal is not performing economic activity, whereas if she were hired to cook a similar meal in a restaurant she would be. This conception of 'economic' excludes activity within the family, and a political struggle waged by 'economic classes' would exclude women, except in their role as wage earners. Socialist and communist movements in the developed countries have also understood economy in this way … when they have talked of political struggle between economic classes, they have essentially excluded women, both the family and housewives, from revolutionary politics." (*Capitalism, the Family and Personal Life*, 1973)

The most direct result of this observation was to redefine women's "consumptive" work in the home as productive, because even if it didn't directly contribute to the accumulation of profit, it laid the foundations for it. The "wages for housework" campaign was, and still is, inspired by the principle that the only way to upgrade women's "free" labour is to pay for it. After all, men pay for prostitutes, housekeepers and cleaners – why not for wives?

The corollary of making domestic work acceptable was that feminists challenged the home "as the woman's domain". The backbone of the 1970s "alternative" movement and socialist/feminist groups like Big Flame aimed to get the men back in the kitchen in order to free women to participate equally in waged labour. Ironically, one of the side effects of the 1970s anti-housework debate is that brand of American feminism where "real women" go out to work and pay for a home help. One class of liberation at the expense of another.

The echoes of the housewife debate were picked up by the feminist health movement. Books like *Our Bodies Ourselves* and *Fat is a Feminist Issue* pointed the way: like fatted geese, they argued, women are bred to consume – either on their own behalf or for the family. In *Fat is a Feminist Issue*, Susie Orbach demonstrated brilliantly the ways in which women rebel against the strictures of their role, either through over or underconsuming. Fat and anorexia became physical conditions and political statements; personal consumption was on the cards as a matter for debate. As Orbach commented: "Compulsive eating is a very painful and, on the surface, self-destructive activity. But feminism has taught us that activities that appear to be self-destructive are invariably adaptions, attempts to cope with the world."

The threat of consumption was picked up in a different way by feminists working in the field of semiology. Judith Williamson's *Decoding Advertisements* and Ros Coward's *Female Desire* both address the way in which women are encouraged to "consume" images, signs and signifiers. We, the audience, "consume" meanings, and in so doing are able to interpret, complete the message of advertising. In the act of ingestion, we discover ourselves, find meaning in our lives and – crucially – pace our lives through the purchase of products. Arguably this is a process which men experience as well. But the crucial point made by Coward is that women are more vulnerable to the process because their upbringing and social expectations define them as consumers and as images to be "consumed" by the gaze of men. Consumption, in this context, verges on cannibalism. "To be a woman is to be constantly addressed, to be constantly scrutinised, to have our desire constantly courted – in the kitchen, on the streets, in the world of fashion, in films and fiction... Desire is endlessly defined and stimulated. Everywhere female desire is sought, bought, packaged and consumed."

British political thought is well aware, then, of the problems created by consumption. Consumption is seen as a threat to socialist and feminist health. Feminists have categorised it as part and parcel of patriarchal oppression, whilst the Labourites, themselves die-hard patriarchs, have chucked the rubber in a different direction. According to orthodox Marxist interpretation, consumption is not part of political economy. The question of exactly who is responsible for consumption, its evils and its political potential, has rarely been asked. At least not in this country.

4: Function and symbolism

The point being made is that what we think of advertising, the value we attach to it as a form of communication, as a way of symbolising the power of commodities, must depend on the importance we attach to the act of consumption.

It can be seen, conversely, that what we think about consumption, what's a good thing to buy, is coloured by advertising. The result of this turkey/egg situation is that we can't think about commodities without holding a silver cross up at the image of advertising, and equally can't discuss the importance of media communication without leering guiltily in the direction of the creaking supermarket shelves.

The unholy marriage between purchasing decisions and advertising is summed up neatly by Douglas Kellner in "Critical Theory, Commodities and the Consumer Society" (*Theory, Culture and Society*, Vol. 1, no. 3, 1983) Kellner does a brilliant salvage job on the socialist's right to buy wheaties or an electric typewriter as part of a new world consumer policy – at the expense of advertising. According to Kellner, we have the right to flounce around in a new seasonal outfit – as long as we patronise a co-op in favour of a big corporation. Given capital's profit mongering and worker exploitation, this makes sense, but Kellner's real gripe against "big money" organisations is their capacity to invest in "manipulative" advertising. He warns from the pulpit: "The corporation is often more concerned with packaging, marketing and advertising than with the quality of the product itself, or whether anyone really needs it ... we should not buy products advertised on television because the extremely costly advertising expenses are passed on to the consumer in the form of higher prices and, secondly, if one really needed and wanted the products advertised on television one would purchase them without needing to be cajoled and manipulated by TV advertising."

The problem with this assumption is that "need" is a "natural" experience, something we know in our chromosomes without access to information, advertising, etc. He also makes that age-old mistake of assuming that "a good quality" product will sell itself. As many products will illustrate (including those produced by "right-on" co-ops and collectives), unless a need is defined, unless a market is created, unless a desire is stimulated, mould and dust will consume the commodity before a punter gets the chance. This, then, is the nub of the problem. Much of the avarice and viciousness associated with advertising is premised on the assumption of natural needs and necessary goods. Necessary goods don't need to be advertised because, tautologically – they are necessary.

Very few writers have entered the hornet's nest of socialist consumer politics: what the children of the revolution will be wearing over their under-pants or under the duvet. Will stiletto heels become museum relics of the Dark Ages? Will lipstick exist? How many different types of car will be on the market? Will the people's car replace the other several hundred models?

Douglas Kellner commented on this problem whilst attacking Herbert Marcuse's pessimistic view of the future: "The problem with Marcuse's account is that he seems to assume that all consumer needs are false and that all commodities are tools of capitalist manipulation... I propose that we carefully scrutinise the commodity world to discern which commodities are useful, which are useless, which are beneficial, which are harmful... In this way we can distinguish between true and false needs and worthless and valuable commodities. Some of these distinctions can be made on a societal level, where a socialist society, for instance, could democratically and rationally decide that 114 models of cars and eighty-nine brands of toothpaste were unnecessary. Other evaluations and discriminations must be made by the individual. I may, for instance, genuinely need and benefit from a new word processor."

The image of a squad of "right-on" socialists voting out tummy button brushes as a waste of resources is very warming, but the problem with Kellner's vision is that he perceives a future inhabited by "rational" peole who make sensible, logical decisions. As we saw earlier in this book, the battle between rational and passionate man is nothing new: it has divided political philosophy from the seventeenth century onwards. To its credit, feminism has played a major part in pinning rational man – arguing for the liberation of emotion, feeling, symbolism and the power of imagination. And mainstream socialist thinking has paid lip service to the feminist outrage that emotion should not be interpreted as hysterics. But the argument has not yet extended from the revolutionary hearth to the revolutionary check-out counter. We may love and breed irresponsibly with passion, but we shouldn't let it inspire an affair with the supermarket.

It's also worth reminding ourselves of the symbolic importance of commodities. As Mike Featherstone explains: "The meaning of goods cannot ... be understood by reference to their intrinsic qualities or predetermined use, rather they become subjected to a continual process of symbolisation and resymbolisation." ("Consumer Culture" in *Theory, Culture and Society*, Vol.1, no.3, 1983) It's possible to turn this pejorative observation around. If goods have no predetermined use outside of symbolisation and meaning being created under a capitalist system, then why should we assume that the power and importance of symbolism should "wither away" under socialism? Maybe, as feminists have argued with reference to the lives of women, the power of emotion, of passion, of desire, should not be excluded from the political equation. And just because people displace the emptiness of their alienated lives by filling up their cupboards from the supermarket trolley, does not detract from the fact that objects are capable of performing important symbolic functions in our lives.

The only people on the broad left to grasp this basic fact – the importance of *symbolism in use* – are the so-called "deviant" sociologists, the people who, with anthropological fervour, observe the "tribal" behaviour of society's outcasts: punks with safety pins through their noses, Teds in full Edwardian evening dress. In an advanced capitalist economy where basic needs of food, clothing and shelter are met (although less so under Thatcher), "commodity as symbol" becomes a crucial ingredient in the ways people display individuality and decorate their lives.

From a radical point of view the crime, the symbol of alienation, is the expression of self through commodity. We, flesh and blood, are no more than the object with which we identify. It's hard to challenge this. In an alienated economy with hordes of the population unemployed or engaged in alienating labour, then what we consume, how we spend our leisure, how we represent our existence to ourselves

through purchasing decisions, is little more than balm on the wound. Slick packaging patches and retreads us for another day. This is the cult of consumerism, the object obsessed world. For, contrary to popular opinion, the crime of advertising is not its ability to play on people's desires and fantasies. Arguably art, literature and culture also do that. Rather, it is the subtle substitution of an object for a dissatisfaction. Consumption becomes a displacement and a solution. The image is pleasurable in its own right, not an incentive to action, but rather an alternative to it.

This option as no option is described by Janice Winship in her profile of *Options* magazine (*Theory, Culture and Society*, p.47). Referring to the sections on fashion, food and homecare and health, she says: "This 'choice' is intimately bound into an ideology of individuality and the latter... is inseparably linked in the magazine content to consumption. Consumption, however, is not only the key to choice but is the practice of individuality and choice... a glowing optimism that women can choose and can determine their own lives... while optimism is no bad thing, modelled as it is in *Options* on the possibilities proffered by commodities and the promise of individuality, it is a very limited optimism."

Consumerism, however, is not the same as consumption

THE FACE No. 68

DECEMBER 1985 90p US $2.95

THE FACE

WEST

THIS IS CHINA'S TOP MODEL
SHE EARNS £50 A MONTH. TEN
YEARS AGO SHE WOULD HAVE
BEEN THROWN IN JAIL . . .

Morris Day

Jeffrey Archer

Womacks

Doug E. Fresh

John Galliano

Swing Out Sister

London Collections

Susan Tully

Photo Pierre Hurel

**UNTOLD WEALTH, UNTOLD STORIES.
INSIDE THE LIVES OF DURAN DURAN**

We are back in Coventry. It is lunchtime, in a pub. Billy is talking to an older trade unionist about the 1920's, the war years, the basic reasoning for union solidarity, and the need for concerted union efforts in 1986 to reverse the faults of the government.

A montage of city life: of people walking in the park; eating their lunch, working. In conversation and song Billy argues the politics is not just about the way we vote or organise at work. It can also have a personal dimension, colouring our view of the world, and influencing how we behave with each other: The politics of love, as in THE SATURDAY BOY.

or, for that matter, use. Useful goods – as the punks have shown – are not necessarily "necessary". Punks didn't "need" safety pins, but they were useful, partly because they held together two sections of clothing and partly because they had an easily identifiable – and challengeable – social meaning. Safety into sadism, nappies into nightmares: a vision of perverted, punctured childhood.

Mass culture as re-usable and disposable, consumption as other than dictated by the billboards, is one of the reasons why sociologists fell in love with sub-cultures. Their very existence testified to the fact that rampant consumerism could be challenged. Culture, sodden with symbolism, could be consumed in a powerful and political way.

The "enfant terrible" of this culture cannibalism is *The Face* magazine, essentially a catalogue of alternative lifestyle, a vision of cultural consumption (music, fashion, dis-information) severed from a clear sense of the economy. The transitory look, the image, is all important. Dick Hebdige commented on this empty political horizon: "This is where *The Face* fits. This is the world where the ideal reader of *The Face* – stylepreneur, doleocrat, Buffalo Boy or Sloane – educated, streetwise but not institutionalised – is learning how to dance in the dark, how to survive, how to stay on top (on the surface) of

things. After all, in 1983 with the public sector, education, the welfare state – all the big 'safe' institutions – up against the wall, there's nothing good or clever or heroic about going under. When all is said and done why bother to think deeply when you're not paid to think deeply?" (*10.8*, no.19)

The Face therefore represents the acceptable face of disaffection, of a youth élite bordering affluent poverty who have no respect for the material values of bourgeois society. Why work hard when there is no work? Why depend on tomorrow when you can go to a night club tonight? Think for the image. *Face* readers consume, but in terms of mainstream media they see themselves as a counter-culture, running against the grain of acceptability. From the point of view of the left's theory of advertising, this also challenges the assumption that the effect of advertising is to turn people into "passive", mindless consumers. It rejects the role of the media as a brainwashing device, and argues that through resistance, people use commodities to their own advantage, to create their own style, not to "live out" the world purveyed by advertising.

Four useful anchor points can be gleaned from deviance studies. First, that the consumer isn't passive. Second, that commodities have no fixed meaning as determined by advertising, packaging or

Picture opposite:

Old adverts and nostalgic graphic styles have become part of the language of contemporary political propaganda. The Power in the Union pamphlet aimed to promote union's interest in the power and potential of the media as an offensive weapon. The first assault would be a film featuring the songs of Billy Bragg, a political song writer who spearheaded The Red Wedge tour in the winter of early 1986. The aim was to forge a connection between the youth movement, Labour politics and the media.

corporate capitalism. Thirdly, that symbolism is as important as functionality in determining the "use" of a product. And finally that consumption is not reducible to consumerism. And if symbolism is as important a part of use as anthropology, deviance studies and the semiologists would suggest, then advertising cannot be blamed for creating "false" images of "real" goods. Commodities must carry with them a shadow of imagination. The issue is more a question of whether we like or can politically accept the kinds of images which modern advertising purveys. As the GLC versus cigarette advertising argument conveys, the advertising technique – the capacity to form people's minds and desires – can be used to good and bad effect. It is part of the "job" of advertising to give products (and consumers) identities and uses. It should be part of a political economy's function to discuss the construction of use, consumer preference and taste.

Instead of this much needed theory, however, political economists and semiologists are guilty of "slipping" between a discussion of value, and one of use. The first job of a radical advertising practice is to dissolve these myths. Product value and consumer use are not the same thing. And in the conflation of terms, one crucial ingredient is missing. That of genuine choice.

5: The right to choose

One of the major faults of advertising as currently commercially practised is that it restricts real choice (in terms of desire and practicality) between competing goods. It forecloses options, militates against criticism and hardly facilitates freedom of information. For several reasons modern advertising does not enable us to make proper choices in the market place:

1. The myth of a country peopled by small corner grocers selling their wares in the market place is smashed by the domination of multinationals and monopolies.

2. The choice which advertising gives us, like the supermarket shelf, is frequently between different brands from the same company.

3. Price is not an indication of "free" democratic competition, but of the power of monopolies to maintain high price levels, or occasionally to undercut smaller outfits to maintain their monopoly.

4. The lack of genuine information about "how" to consume means that consumers are prey to the seductions of the more punitive forms of advertising, with occasional struggles to "improve" our

capacity to make educated purchasing decisions, for example over food additives.

5. Choice between commodities is also perverted by a dominant form of advertising logic which relies on the Achilles heel of frustration, depression, poverty and ambition to sell products.

Socialist economic debates often emphasise the fact that capitalism provides us with too many similar goods from which to choose. If most of these goods are unnecessary, and most of the choices specious, then the assumption is that, under socialism, we would consume less. But "social democratic" decision making can only be interpreted as State decision making, legislative bodies given the power to vote over the fate of toothpaste or the availability of coloured durex to the population. So far, socialism hasn't had to put this to the test. If Western capitalism is dogged by a crisis of over-production, continually inciting the worker to consume more, the socialist countries such as Cuba and the USSR are characterised by long queues for even the most basic of commodities.

I've tried to argue that removing advertising will not automatically cut the craving for a range of commodities, and that what is necessary in life can no more be deduced from the back of a packet than from an ouija board. Use and need is informed by communication and information. Symbolism and artifice is as much a human sanctuary as "logic", and whether reinforced by advertising or not, commodities will continue to fulfil those functions.

Necessary and unnecessary goods cannot be decided by a State quango, now or in the future. Nor will unnecessary goods automatically fade away once the marketing plug is pulled. Nor, for that matter, will necessary goods automatically get to the people who want them unless a sophisticated and imaginative communications network is maintained. Everybody knows that the "worthy but dull" maxim and "It'll do you good" never sold anything apart from patent medicine. Choice, the fostering of individual desires and preferences in the consumer field, the right to use commodities as we wish, has to stay. And one of the implications of that is that the market place, as an arena for making decisions, also has to stay.

To suggest this is to fly in the face of traditional Marxist analysis, which argues that the egalitarian nature of the market place is a myth: only those with the money can make "free" decisions, and commercial monopolies in turn rig the decision-making stakes. Choosing a loaf invariably means choosing between remakes of Mother's Pride, choosing sugar means choosing Tate and Lyle. However, as the authors of *What A Way To Run A Railroad* (Landry and others, Comedia, 1985) point out:

"It is time to recognize that market mechanisms have progressive political possibilities as an index of social needs. The proviso is that one must bear in mind that the information that the market can give you on needs is always limited by existing distribution of wealth and income. What the market can tell you about is effective demand at a given price. Thus, needs which people have but cannot afford to meet at given prices, will be invisible. However, this limitation derives from the inequitable distribution of wealth under capitalism. To the extent that socialist development reduces the scale of that inequality, to that same extent this limitation on the 'feedback' that market mechanisms can give about needs is reduced.

For us, the market is not some mystical religion to which every area of life should correspond, but simply the most practical way of gaining information about the thousands of complex choices users make about goods and services. Clearly, in some areas, it ceases to have much value as a term and for these areas we do not pretend that it operates as a useful mechanism."

What is clear from the downward drift in the left's popularity is that the so-called "political alternative" has little understanding of how the people, the voters, think or function. Their desires are a mystery, their living patterns hypothetical and beliefs misunderstood. Nowhere is the gulf in popular consciousness more apparent than in the arena of consumption. And yet "finding out what people want" is an essential ingredient of democracy.

As we've seen in earlier chapters, market research depends on the pre-classification of people into groups, structured by occupation, sex and age. These three determinants are thought to give the best guide to social aspiration and, as a consequence, patterns of consumption. In other words, marketing recognises social ideology as having a material effect on the ways in which people spend their money. The left, still battling in a mire of political economy, hasn't even got this far.

More than "leaving the Devil all the best tunes", the left is actually guilty of allowing advertising, on occasions, to develop a more sophisticated understanding of capitalism and consumer motives than it has at its own command. In short, the left needs to reap the benefits of the market research industry: it needs to develop a theory of the consumer fleshed out by the fictions which people carry in their heads as well as the facts produced in sheets of statistics. Whether this is done by a market research team, a MORI poll or a local community group, the principle is the same: effective communication and the potential for change depend on knowledge of the consumer. After all, if they were people who thought like "us" we wouldn't be talking to them in the first place!

6: Dressing up: advertising and propaganda

If the left can be accused of not taking account of the consumer, it can also be accused of not creating images for its ideas which are "appealing". As we've seen, the problem has been gearing itself up to the era of communications. In the last general election this was partly out of political distrust for the media, partly from a genuine belief that the "old" doorstep methods were best. As Simon Hoggart commented at the time on Michael Foot: "Many politicians tend to think TV doesn't really matter. [But] even if a thousand people a day see Foot speak in person during the campaign, they will total no more than 0.05% of the population, a tiny fragment of those who will watch him on TV." (*The Observer*, 24.4.1983) Even if this distrust is overcome, we've seen that the prohibitive costs of using advertising and the media effectively bar all but the most affluent campaigning groups. The sheer cost of the GLC campaign, for example, (£10–11 million in total) makes it unlikely that many left groups will be able to take immediate advantage of commercial advertising.

But putting money to one side for the moment, the whole emphasis of this book has been on the ways in which the left discredits the rhetoric and image of advertising: the magic system which appeals to and undermines our emotions. The idea that appealing to the emotions is "bad" is clearly as fallacious as the assumption that "good" propaganda only appeals on rational grounds. It is also a kind of minimalist thinking which finds no place for political art, theatre or fiction.

Clearly a difference between propaganda and advertising does exist. Advertising is usually associated with the selling of commodities, propaganda with politics. But from Dwight Eisenhower through to the GLC it is clear that advertising can be employed very well in a propaganda function. Nor, for that matter, does the difference lie in origin. It rests on "intention" and, in the end, profit. Whose interests are served by the campaign? "Good" political advertising/propaganda serves to ask questions: it aims to democratise the mind of the reader. This "opening up" of the debate applies equally well to Heartfield's anti-fascist montages and the GLC's anti-Tory campaign. And this idea of "opening up" debate clearly differentiates "good" advertising from the bulk of commercial campaigns, which function on the principle of exclusion.

But finding a role for advertising also goes hand in hand with finding an acceptable role for consumption. It means taking the "alternative" economy's obsession with second-hand goods to the laundry. Under fire from the factories to consume new dishwashers, cookers, clothes and books, the left takes refuge in the second-hand thrift shops and jumble palaces. Rarely is this preference expressed on the grounds of cost, and Britain's alternative economy – comprised of disparate feminists, gays, socialists, Labourites, non-aligned Greens and de-centralised hippies – consumes second-hand goods as a matter of principle. Barter consumption is a convenient let-out clause, a way of not confronting the exploitation of labour invested in "cheap" imports, or of making decisions about what should be manu-factured.

It follows from this that "what" is being promoted or sold does matter. Whilst I've been keen to abandon the distinction between "use value"

and "exchange value", necessary and unnecessary goods, natural and unnatural needs, it's important to retain some sense of value. The point is, whether we want a good, or need it, should be a social and ultimately political decision, not a biological one.

The same principle applies to the creation of the advertising image. As *City Limit*'s Roy Patterson pointed out, the act of placing an ad is in itself political. If the magazine deems an image offensive to its readers, it negotiates with the agency to change it. The fact that advertising uses "false" illusory lifestyles and sexual stereotypes, does not automatically discredit the function of advertising. Rather, it raises the question of how to create new images which are seductive and sell the kind of values the left has faith in.

Unfortunately, the idea of "aesthetic" ugliness, that only the truly awful tells the truth, has taken firm root in the foundations of socialism. It is premised on an assumption that the visually pleasing conceals, and that art para-lyses not politicises. It assumes that in the final analysis, form and function are divisible, and that style is the icing on the cake.

The challenge to this "mud and guts" philosophy, has come from within the left. From the Frankfurt School onwards there has been a battle over the image, a belief that political art must inspire as well as inform. Clive Dilnot, in an unpublished paper, challenged the commonsense distinction between design, commodities and "real needs". "Since 1945 it has been impossible to maintain these distinctions. There have been no projects and no practices constructed since 1945 which have not been formed within a web of existing economic relations, there are no levels of the satisfaction or the meeting of material needs which are not implicated in economic relations and there are no cultural products, in an era when the economic has itself become cultural, and culture is an industry, that are not simultaneously items in the inventory of contemporary political economy." (*Design, Industry and The Economy since 1945*, 1983) The point is a simple one, and one that's been made repeatedly. Design, culture, tastes and preferences are part of a political economy. This applies to the fruits of capitalism and, by extension, must apply to the seeds of socialism. The cultural is not peripheral to the economic.

Conclusion

One solution is quite clear. The GLC used the language of capitalism against itself. They used advertising to subvert the system both aesthetically and economically.

But whilst subversion can be one of the most effective methods of discrediting a political position, by itself it cannot create "new" languages of communication. It can only respond and counter attack; subversion is guerilla aesthetics. It is primarily defensive.

It is no accident that precisely at the time when the Labour Party and the left in general is cranking itself up to the imperative of creating something new, prising itself off the barricades, is the time when the Tory Party with all the anger of a mutilated buffalo has stormed into the offensive. The Local Government Bill, due to become law in the Spring of 1986, represents the front line. By defining all critical information and advertising as subversive propaganda, it seeks to emasculate the opposition and silence it, thus threatening the foundations of a "free society" and an information democracy, in a high-tec world where knowledge is power.

But the implications of the Tory offensive run much deeper than a silencing of dissent. Since the War the appeal of Conservative politics has been its monopoly on commonsense. It offers to conserve, to protect that which we have. It defines itself not as an ideology but as a lifestyle. Conservatism is not so much a belief, a mental state, as a way of life. It is built out of bricks and mortar, green fields and fully automatic washing machines. The world which it purports to represent is material, stable and, ultimately, available in the local supermarket. It is papered by brave new wallpaper, holiday brochures and HP payments: an object-filled Never-Never-Land.

And this appeal is, rightly so, the ultimate threat for the left. Rather than grappling head on with the seduction and necessity of commodities, it ridicules their importance, castigates their owners and seeks to censor their existence. The left lives in a post-apocalyptic twilight where second-hand goods are bartered with black market zeal, and where the only secure vision is a half forgotten, hopelessly nostalgic memory of the past. It revels drunkenly in the hand-me-down sentiments and grimy thumbed pages of the workers' movement in the 1930s. A horrid, sordid epoch when hunger marches filled the streets, rancid tea filled the belly and rickets filled the classroom. And because the workers, starved and pummelled into resistance, complained and dreamed of a better world, Labour colonised this slaughterhouse of a decade, renaming it the Holy Wars, Nirvana, the promised land.

And if this sad, soggy truth weren't enough, it appropriated the heady post-War victory as its own. Revelling in the fact that at last "the people" saw the light and opposed the inequality which had bitten deep into the flesh of its children. Wanton historical amnesia possessed the young socialists, obliterating the fact that it was the War, not the Labour Party, which changed people's hearts, and that the liberal Conservative philanthropy of Beveridge and Keynes did more to establish the Welfare State than the Labour Party or the trade unions.

For what the left lacked was not morality, nor credibility, but vision. So busy with righting the wrongs of the moment, fighting for better working conditions and wages, it forgot its purpose, its path into tomorrow. It lacked a Utopia with which to inspire the hearts and minds of the people. It lacked any alternative world other than that already presented and cemented by the Tory vision of fitted carpets, three-piece suites, harsh brash cars and a place in the country called "Little England" or "Home Sweet Home".

The poverty of imagination, this obsession with the brass tacks of wage negotiations and defending the shit pittance of everyday life was suffocating. And whilst the boys slogged it out on the picket lines and the girls defended their right to stay housewives, as long as they were paid for it, the Wilson White Heat Revolution of the 1960s lay in ruins: a powder puff version of socialism furnished with debts, inflation and an endless production line of cheaply upholstered cars. Meanwhile, with the country in a state of disaffection, its dreams ruptured by the failure of May 1968, the people waited with baited breath and open arms for the Conservatives, rekindling the sweet memory of Macmillan and "You never had it so good" consumerism. And the Tory government, revelling in the smelted remains of the white heat treatment, stealthily crept up through the late 1960s and early 1970s, saw a glimpse of a glittering land gilded with goodies and greed, and called this cash-and-carry country Jerusalem.

And whilst the Conservatives swept up and down the aisles of the supermarkets, gathering disciples, the Labour Party, with the insistence of Jeremiah, forgot about Wilson and reminded people about the tyranny of unemployment, ill health, poor education and their servitude of the State. It asked for a revolution, offering not homes for heroes, but a vapid, vascillating vision of Nothing.

Much has changed in the last three years since the Labour Party wore its heart on its sleeve and sackcloth and ashes on its back, parading its election failure before a country swamped by the jubilant Britannia side-show called Thatcherism. The left has, with Luddite grace, picked up on the importance of advertising and "effective" communication. And the GLC, if it achieved nothing else, exposed the Tory myth, arresting trade unions and that vast dissenting people that identifies itself as the left, to the importance of using, not being used by, the media.

Advertising is an expensive business: glossy commercials don't come cheap, but the *principles* of expertise and marketing analysis are there to be gleaned. All the more important in an era when the right is as much concerned with decimating the enemy as with winning. Advertising is a metaphor for the age. Used and abused as the key to private profits, it still provides the most sophisticated economic and ideological analysis of the desires, aims and ambitions of that strife-torn plunder pit called Britain. It provides a method for understanding the link between images and Utopias, occupation and ambition, class and culture, commodities and capitalism. It provides an analysis which is, by definition, political. The left ignores that at its peril.

Bibliography

Adams, Carol and Laurikietis, Rae, *The Gender Trap: Book 3, Messages and Images*, Virago, 1976.

Barker, Paul, ed, *Art in Society*, Fontana, 1977.

Bennett, Compton, *Poster and Showcards*, Foulsham, 1930.

Bishop, F. P., *The Ethics of Advertising*, Robert Hale, 1949.

Brewster and Palmer, *Introduction to Advertising*, McGraw Hill, 1935.

Buckman, Peter, *All for Love*, Secker and Warburg, 1984.

Coward, Rose, Lipshitz, Sue and Cowie, Elizabeth, "Psychoanalysis and Patriarchal Structures", in *Papers in Patriarchy*, 1976.

Coward, Rose, *Female Desire*, Granada, 1984.

Dyer, Gillian, *Advertising as Communication*, Methuen, 1982.

Gambles, A. and Walton, P., *Capitalism in Crisis*, Macmillan, 1976.

Golden, Robert, *Photography and Politics One*, The Photography Workshop, 1979.

Kempner, Macmillan and Hawkins, *Business and Society*, Pelican, 1974.

King, Josephine and Stott, Mary, *Is This Your Life? Images of Women in the Media*, Virago, 1977.

Landry, Charles, Morley, David, Southwood, Russell and Wright, Patrick, *What a Way to Run A Railroad*, Comedia, 1985.

Mayer, Martin, *Madison Avenue USA*, Penguin, 1958.

Packard, Vance, *The Hidden Persuaders*, Pelican, 1962.

Packard, Vance, *The Waste Makers*, Pelican, 1960.

Whyte, William H., *The Organisation Man*, Penguin, 1960.

Williams, Raymond, *Problems in Materialism and Culture*, 1980.

Williamson, Judith, *Decoding Advertisements*, 1978.

Zaretsky, Eli, *Capitalism, The Family and Personal Life*, 1973.

Other titles from Comedia

Organizations and Democracy Series

No. 1 **WHAT A WAY TO RUN A RAILROAD — an analysis of radical failure** by Charles Landry, David Morley, Russell Southwood and Patrick Wright
£2.50 paperback

No. 2 **ORGANIZING AROUND ENTHUSIAMS: Patterns of Mutual Aid in Leisure** by Jeff Bishop and Paul Hoggett
£4.95 paperback

No. 3 **BAD SOLUTIONS TO GOOD PROBLEMS: The Practice of Organizational Change** by Liam Walsh
£3.95, due Spring 1987